The 14½lb Budgie

Also in Arrow by Mike Harding

*The Unluckiest Man in the World
and Similar Disasters
The Armchair Anarchist's Almanac
Killer Budgies
When the Martians Land in Huddersfield*

The 14½lb Budgie

Mike Harding

Illustrated by Chic Jacob

Arrow Books

Arrow Books Limited
62-65 Chandos Place, London WC2N 4NW

An imprint of Century Hutchinson Ltd

London Melbourne Sydney Auckland
Johannesburg and agencies throughout
the world

First published by Robson Books 1980
Arrow edition 1981
Reprinted 1982, 1983, 1984 and 1985 (twice)

Set in Linoterm Times by
Book Economy Services, Cuckfield, Sussex

Printed and bound in Great Britain by
Anchor Brendon Limited, Tiptree, Essex

ISBN 0 09 926540 0

*For Pat, Sarah and Emma who
gave me a reason for doing it –
poverty – and for Morag who
manages to make sense out of
most of the things I do.*

Contents

Mike Harding

Born October 1944 in Crumpshall, Manchester. Upon hearing of this, Hitler immediately takes to bunker brauned off. Trained by Irish grandmother in the ancient Gaelic art of breathing.

Aged 4 becomes leader of local Guy Fawkes cult.

Aged 5 leads neighbourhood guerillas in raid on Green Hand Gang Headquarters in disused Kosher bacon warehouse. Loses rubber dagger, and Bat Man mask and is wounded by spud gun in skirmish.

Age 7 becomes leader of Theresa Murphy appreciation society, but is forced to abdicate post when discovered playing 'doctors and nurses' in disused Kosher bacon warehouse by Mr and Mrs Murphy.

Between ages of 11 and 18 attends St Bede's Catholic School, Manchester where education (previously having consisted solely of Dan Dare, Three Stooges and Wilson the Athlete) is broadened to include 'O'-Level Sin and Damnation.

Leaves school confirmed atheist with doubts on dark nights and Christmas Day morning. Takes to road as musician during beat boom. Ravaged by groupies and eventually marries one to found 17th Harding Dynasty. Later goes on to Folk Clubs and stardom.

Has been drunk in most countries in world and is hangover champion of six continents.

Barks a lot and shaves four times a day during periods of full moon.

Still refuses to leave the spiritual womb of the North of England (real ale, fog, pie and peas etc.) for promises of knighthoods and mucky women in London. Has written plays, stories, novels, poetry and begging letters in a vain attempt to escape the painful world of comedy, all to no avail.

Chic Jacob

This intrepid southern grandad travelled North (throwing all caution to the wind – and subsequently getting a lot of it) to research atmosphere for most of these drawings; almost retreated in the face of a heavy onslaught of black puddings, tripe and onions, mushy peas, chip butties and Uncle Joe's mint balls; saved face by supping ale for ale with gnarled northern journalists in that splendid little Wilson's pub up Great Ancoats Street – enthralling them with tales of his escapades when Chief Escape Officer in Fleet Street's grim Black Lubianka (two successful home runs).

One-time evacuee (ringside seat for the Battle of Britain), farmhand, shepherd, ploughman and muckspreader. Saw wartime service in South-East Asia (Acting Able Seaman – Non-Substantiated), where single-handed he held an emergency exit door when two thousand mutinous matelots attempted a mass breakout from the Royal Naval Cinema, Colombo (where he was Second-in-Command), during a showing of the all-action British movie _Champagne Charlie_, thereby averting what might have been one of the greatest disasters ever to hit the British film industry.

Some Perfunctory Answers to the Question 'Why?'

People ask me why I do what I do. . . . The simple answer, I suppose, is that I took a look at myself and at the world around me, put down my pint and my fag (I was four at the time), and I remember thinking distinctly, as my gran was sat by the fire cleaning the cat with her Black and Decker . . . 'Either the world is mad or I am', and I suppose I've spent the rest of my life trying to work out which side of the proposition approximates closer to the truth.

Born in the picturesque fishing village of Crumpsall-on-Irk at a time when bombs were falling like second-hand car salesmen's promises, I spent the formative years of my life in an air-raid shelter papered with my gran's old copies of the *African Missionary Magazine*. A lot of the pictures on the pages showed bare-chested African ladies dancing and my gran, being a right-minded and banshee-fearing person, had scratched the pointed bits out. As a result of this (until I was twenty-one and bought a book on dressmaking), I thought that all ladies had bricked-up chests.

We were so poor that I remember with vivid clarity the first time I saw a butcher's shop. We were walking down the road, my mother and I, on my way to see how my dad had done at the local pub's 'Best Liar to Dole Clerks' competition, when this butcher's shop window caught my eye. I'd never seen meat before, thought it was an accident and rang for an ambulance, and spent more than half an hour giving first aid to a sheet of spare ribs.

I suppose the most important person to me during these formative years was my Uncle Festus Beauregard Dipfinger. Uncle Festus would come out with memorable sayings at the drop of a flat-cap. Things like . . .

'It's a long road that has no turnips.'

'If work was in bed I'd sleep on the floor.'

'A man who tests see-saws has an up-and-down sort of life.'

'Don't blame the dog – you trod in it.'

It was sayings like this and the fond memory of him rattling the bars of his cage defiantly at the sergeant when he was had up for a political offence (he broke into the Conservative Club on the corner) . . . yes, it was memories like these that sustained me through the long years and the hard times to come like playing . . .

Dundee . . . the town that invented the coffin

Egremont . . . where the tide hopes it doesn't have to come in

Birmingham . . . the town that looks as though it was designed by a Lego salesman

Bridlington Pavilion . . . a vegetarian slaughterhouse

Todmorden Town Hall . . . a Chinese bomb shelter

Bradford Alhambra . . . a theatre so old they found Valentino's camel still living in the boiler room.

Still, it's not been a hard life . . . and when I think back on the old days . . . gran doing seven shifts a week down the zip-fastener mines . . . grandad helping her on with her moustache and boots in the morning . . . my sister happily ironing British Rail surplus sandwiches flat again. We were happy but poor – so poor, in fact, that one Christmas when we'd run out of coal our Sid sucked a mint, and we all warmed our hands on his tongue. We couldn't afford soup, so me mam thickened some rainwater . . . it was like drinking smoke.

I remember how ugly I was as a child . . . when I was a baby my pram was rented from Hammer Films. . . . I had a job frightening the other kids in the street to bed and my ears stuck out so much that from the back I looked like a wing nut. . . . I remember my mother tried sticking them back with glue and plaster and fly paper, but as I grew bigger the tension caused by having my ears still stuck back gave me a permanent maniac smile – *rictus lunaticus* – that caused old women to bless themselves and boosted the sale of crucifixes and garlic in our area tremendously.

I remember the Coronation Party we had in our street most clearly . . . the bunting we had stolen from the Town Hall laid out along the house fronts gently wafting in the breeze from the glue factory, cleverly concealing Grandma McClusky's window-box full of senna pod plants. . . .

I remember all the screaming, happy kids, stuffing themselves with potted-paste sandwiches and asking philosophical questions such as *'Whyzeegomorrenme?'* which usually received a reply such as *'Shutyerfaceralshurritferyer'*.

Into these troubled but happy waters came a small, grubby, cherubic figure with a question on his pouting lips.

'*Mrs,*' he enquired of an elderly crone who was spooning out a suspicious-looking gritty substance that went under the vague and not entirely convincing description of trifle – '*Mrs,*' he asked, '*ave yer goranee brown jelly?*'

The aged crone replied to the effect that red jelly they had in the shape of a rabbit; green jelly they had in the shape of the grass around the corpse of said shivering and badly mutilated rodent; yellow jelly they had in the shape of a German paratrooper's helmet, that being the only other mould available . . . but brown jelly they had not.

'*In that case,*' replied the cherub, '*your baby's just ate a tin of brown paint.*'

The 14½lb Budgie

I've got this thing about budgies. I've got a thing about tortoises as well but not as bad as the thing about budgies.

The thing about tortoises is that you can avoid them

unless you get a particularly fast one. But tortoises are
horrible, really, when you look at them. They are like
Vincent Price with a bus shelter on their backs. I picked
up a tortoise once and I shook it and it fell out – they are
really horrible in the nude, like gherkins with legs on.
The only good thing about tortoises is that they make
good pets for dogs with no teeth 'cos you can throw them
and if the dogs don't fetch them back, they can come
back on their own. And at least a tortoise will smile a bit.
You can always see a tortoise grinning a bit when it's
going for a piece of lettuce, if you've got any imagina-
tion. But a budgie never grins. It just sort of sits there all
the time glaring at you and shifting from one leg to
another, muttering.

But I've had this thing about budgies since I was a kid.
We had this budgie when I was a kid and it was the
Khengis Khan of budgies. It was the horribilist budgie in
the whole world. It had torn all its own feathers off so it
looked hard, and it had got a ball point pen and it had
written 'Hell's Angels Cheekie Boy Chapter' on its chest.
Because it had no feathers it couldn't fly, so me dad had
made it a pair of wings out of an old porridge packet and
it used to hang-glide out of the cage and home in on the
hot thermals that were coming off my porridge, and it

19

used to just hang up there on these hot thermals going round and round with its cardboard wings, crapping in my porridge. The thing about budgie muck is that it looks like porridge and me mother never noticed and the budgie used to climb up the pole and lie on the floor of its cage in the sandpaper, laughing and thumping its chest. I've hated budgies ever since.

My second encounter with a budgie was even more traumatic. I was about twenty-one or two at the time, working in a factory making aerosol chips and living in a block of flats in Manchester. Living opposite me was the most beautiful Irish nurse you have ever seen. Two of everything she should have and all in the right place. But I was very shy at the time with no idea how to address women and even less of an idea of how to undress them. I tried to show her that I was interested in her by pulling funny faces and wearing daft party hats every time she went past and putting subtle *billets doux* under her door, saying things like, 'I'd like to give you a punch up the drawers.'

And then one day it happened. In a fit of generosity, she let me carry 4cwt of coal upstairs for her and invited me in for a cup of coffee. This is it, I thought. I went in and sat down on the settee, and she made me a cup of coffee and told me that her name was Pog Mahone. Then a strange eerie feeling crept over me. I knew there was something wrong. The hair stood up on the back of my neck. I broke out into a cold sweat, and then I saw it.

In a specially reinforced cage on the sideboard was a budgie that was even worse than the one we had. It had a patch over one eye, a pirate's hat on, one leg and a crutch and a little man on his shoulder, and it was hobbling about going, 'Pieces of Nine', 'Pieces of Nine'. . . .

I stood up and zoomed out of the flat, and she flew after me, asking, 'What's the matter?'

'Well, I've got this terrible thing – it's claustrophobia.'

'I'm sorry about that because I wanted to ask you a favour,' she said.

'Well, go on then.'

'I was wondering if you would have Christmas dinner with me?'

'That's nice, 'cos I'll be on me own.'

'I'll be on my own as well.'

'Oh,' I said, 'certainly,' because Christmas was only about a fortnight off. Then she said:

'I wanted to ask you one other thing. I've got to go and see me mum and dad in Liverpool. While I'm away, would you mind Attila for me?'

'What?'

'Attila, my little budgie.'

'Oh,' I said, 'I'm not very good with living things. Plastic flowers die on me. The Wellies even fell off my Paddington Bear and he got pneumonia and died.'

'Oh,' she said, 'I don't think you'll have any trouble with Attila, 'cos he loves people. He loved you, I could tell. And all you have to do is feed him, bath him and talk to him.'

'What do you talk to him about.'

'Oh, just tell him about what's gone on during the day,' she said, 'the news or anything like that. He likes to hear news. Read things out of the newspapers.'

I thought, 'Oh, my God, what's happening here?' All I wanted was an uncomplicated relationship with a quick punch up the drawers and down the pub. But I gave in. 'Okay,' I said. And I took the budgie and looked after him for a fortnight.

Now, I'm being totally honest when I say that I would never, ever hurt any living thing on purpose. I looked after that budgie as though it was one of my own. I came in from work, I talked to it, I fed it well. I gave it everything I had – egg and bacon in the morning, meat, two veg and gravy at night. And you know, it never ate it. Just turned its nose up at it. I even bathed it. I felt stupid getting into the bath with a budgie, I can tell you that, scrubbing it down, then drying it with a hair dryer and rubbing its little crutch dry. But I did everything I could. I even ripped up bits of newspaper and put it in its cage so that it had something to read, and do you know what it did? It died out of spite! Definitely. I could see what was running through its mind. It just said one day, 'Right, I'm going to knacker your chances with me mistress.' And he just lay down in the cage and *finito benito*, the wooden overcoat job, 'Come on, Death, let's have it. Thank you very much.' Wham, bam, thank you, mam – gonsky. As far as the David Attenborough stakes were concerned, it was scoring zero on the livometer.

I came home from work and found it there. I tried everything I could. I tried giving it the kiss of life with a pea shooter over its beak. I tried steaming it fresh over the kettle. I even tried the rubber bands up the jacksie and the propeller on the nose but it just kept dive-bombing the floor. In the end I thought there's nothing for it, I'm going to have to get another one.

Now, bear in mind that this was Christmas. I thought, 'Well, you can't walk through the streets of Manchester with a dead budgie sticking out the top of your pocket.' So I got an old Woolies carrier bag and stuck the budgie in the paper bag and went down the street.

On the way, with it being Christmas Eve, the town was going crackers; all the people were in the pubs from the offices getting drunk and insulting the boss. And there I saw a mate of mine, Nobby Carr. He said, 'Mike, come on and have a drink in Yates' Wine Lodge.'

I said, 'Nobby, I got to go to the pet shop.'

'The pet shops are open all day, don't worry about it.'

So, of course, we went into Yates' Wine Lodge giving it six-nowt, plenty of capneb, elbow-bending, milk of amnesia, doom booze, goodnight mother, the Martians have landed. In two hours' time, I'm in no pain at all.

Now what I didn't know was that a bloke had come in and was stood at the side of us drinking and he had an identical Woolies bag. He puts his bag down, has a few bevvies and goes out with my bag, leaving me with a 14½lb oven-ready turkey, in a Woolco carrier bag. Well, I picked it up and thought that it had gone heavy, but I thought maybe that it was just the drink weakening me.

So I went into this pet shop, there's nobody about and I put it on the counter and started talking to the animals. 'Hello, rabbits, hello, piranha fish. Have a rabbit, piranha fish.' And then in came the shopkeeper.

'What do you want, pal?' he asked.

'I want a budgie exactly like that one in the bag.'

'What?'

'There's a dead budgie in that bag belonging to my girl friend. I've got to get her another one for Christmas. Get it changed. Exactly like that one.'

He looked in the bag, looked up, just shook his head, and didn't say very much apart from, 'Exactly like this one?'

'Yeah.'

'We've got a right head-banger here,' he thought.

He went into the back of the shop and what I didn't know, of course, was that in the back he had 3000 turkeys that he had been fattening up for Christmas. And he went into the centre of this big pile of turkeys and pulled out the Al Capone of them all. It had a wing span of 12½ ft. He jammed it in the Woolco bag and sellotaped all the top up so that I couldn't see it. Sold it to me for £25. Well, I got hold of the bag and it was jumping all over the place, this muttering bulk. I said, 'It's a lively bugger, this.'

'Oh aye,' he said, 'you'll get your mileage out of that.'

I went out of the shop and the turkey had kicked its legs out of the bag and it was leading me down the street. Well, I went in this pub for a few bevvies on the way home and this turkey is walking round kicking the landlord's dog and there's blokes looking at it, putting their drinks down and saying, 'That's it. That's the last drink I have. No more booze for me. I've just seen a Woolies carrier bag walking past kicking the landlord's dog.'

Well, I had a few more bevvies and staggered out with this turkey in the bag leading me down the street. And I was Christmas crackered by then, so I rode home on it all the way up the flight of stairs and into the flat.

Now, you wouldn't believe the trouble I had getting it in the cage. It did not want to know. I tried everything. I put down a row of dried peas, tried pecking them myself

up to the door of the cage, showing it. But it did not want to know. In the end, it was down to the vaseline and the brick hammer. I vaselined it all over, gave it one clout with the brick hammer and bang! – it was in. But it did not like it. It jammed its head out of the cage and looked round saying, 'What's happening, what's happening?' Well, I threw a cover over it and left it there. Forgot all about it.

The next morning I woke up with a head like a burglar's dog. There was a knock on the door. It was Pog Mahone. She was back. So I flung open the door and said, 'Happy Christmas,' because of course it was Christmas Day.

'Where's Attila? I bet he's missed his mummy, hasn't he?' she said.

Without thinking, I just pointed over to the corner of the flat. She went over, took the cover off the cage and nearly dropped cork-legged.

'You've been overfeeding him.'

'No, I haven't. I've just been giving him what I had. Egg and bacon.'

Then she saw something that I'd forgotten completely. That one I'd got in the cage had two legs! She said, 'That's not my Attila, you've killed him, you monster!' and flew out of my flat into her own, shut the door and left me on my own. Christmas Day, no Christmas dinner, no food, no party.

'Well, that's it,' I thought.

And the turkey is still looking round the flat, saying, 'What's happening? What's happening?' So I covered it with a cloth again and went off down the pub.

So I'm stood there with this daft party hat on and a meat pie with a piece of holly sticking out of the middle of it and a brandy; I've set fire to it and I'm watching the Queen on the telly when in comes the bloke who took my budgie by mistake the day before. He looks like he's just fought World War III on his own. He's got a black eye, a broken nose, all his teeth missing, half his hair's been torn out, his arm's in plaster of Paris, one of his legs is broken, his suit's flapping in the breeze and he's got one of these blowers with the feather on the end that unwraps and makes a squeaking noise, permanently lodged up his right nostril. Every time he says anything that begins with 'f', this blower unravels itself and squeaks.

So he stands at the bar and says, 'Give me a pint of (wheeping) bitter, please, Jimmy.'

I looked at him and said, 'You've had a good Christmas, pal?'

'Don't talk to me about (wheeping) Christmas. I had a few (wheeping) beers yesterday in Yates' and gets home totally (wheeping) wasted. Well, the wife's at her (wheeping) mother's getting the kids' presents so I thought I'll get the (wheeping) turkey ready. So I opens the (wheeping) bag and if that's a (wheeping) fourteen and a (wheeping) half pound turkey I'm the (wheeping) Pope. I've seen more meat on a (wheeping) butcher's biro. And it isn't even plucked. So it's two o' (wheeping) clock in the (wheeping) morning and I've got the (wheeping) electric razor out and I'm shaving it. Then I've got four pound of (wheeping) stuffing to get in it. In the end it's down to the icing bag up the jacksie. So I've got it stuffed. I lie it there with a little bacon waistcoat and put all the (wheeping) spuds round it. I work it out on the timer – twenty minutes a (wheeping) pound – that's nine times six divided by three, call it ten hours, that's twelve o'clock tomorrow. So I set it, get to (wheeping) feather and crash out. So I wake up this (wheeping) morning. I've got a head like a bucket of frogs, the (wheeping) kids are running round mad.

There's one of them (wheeping) dolls that eats, drinks and wets herself throwing up in the corner, there's a (wheeping) Action Man walking round with a (wheeping) Scalextric out all over the (wheeping) place, up the (wheeping) sideboard, over their granny's head. And sat all round the table is the wife's family all getting (wheeping) smashed on my booze. All the wife's (wheeping) brothers are there, all eleven of them straight out of nick. They're all so (wheeping) hard they make Al Capone look like a poof. The wife's got a face like a box of chisels. She just says, "I've got the (wheeping) veg, get the (wheeping) turkey out of the oven." I open the oven door and you won't believe it. It's lying there like a walnut with three matchsticks. I thought say nowt and they (wheep) all might not notice. I took it in and the brothers thought I was taking the (wheeping) mickey, over goes the (wheeping) table, fuses the (wheeping) Scalextric, the (wheeping) brothers are smashing the place up, in comes the (wheeping) law, knock, knock, bang, bang, 'ello, 'ello, 'ello, thump, thump, nut, nut, boot, boot, bleed, bleed, (wheeping) bracelets and meat wagon and two hundred quid bail, and do you know what I got for Xmas? — a (wheeping) budgie.'

Then I was suddenly thinking. And I'm starting to piece things together, which is not very easy for me at that time in the afternoon after giving it plenty of elbow-bending. And I suddenly thought that maybe that wasn't a budgie in the cage back at the flat. So I went back and I had a look and I decided that it wasn't a budgie. And I got it out of the cage with a sink plunger and I thought I would take it back down and find the bloke and get it changed again. Then maybe I'll be back in Pog Mahone's good books.

So I get it out with the sink plunger, bung it in the bag and offski. On the way I met Nobby again and he said,

'Mike – where are you going?'

'I've got to go round to the pet shop and knock him up,' I said.

'Well,' said Nobby, 'he's not in. He boozes in the Dog and Dilemma over there. We'll go in there and we'll sit down and have a few beers and he'll be in in a bit.'

'Okay,' I said. But he wasn't there.

So we were sitting down having a few beers and playing a game of crib. . . . And I'm sat there and this turkey is between my legs below the seat.

The turkey by now has just about had enough. It's been up and down Manchester in a Woolies carrier bag. It's been shoved in a wire vest, not fed, left for hours on end, been vaselined, brick-hammered and sink-plunged and it's pig-sick. It's in the bag and I'm playing cards and it thinks, 'That's enough.' Bump . . . straight out of the bag, rips the top off, sticks its head right out between my legs – poking out like a periscope, looking round, going, 'Gobble, gobble, gobble . . .'

There's this little old lady sat next to me. And she sees the turkey and says, 'Oooh! Look, Vera . . . this bloke here . . . he's got his "Oh be joyful" out!'

'Well,' says Vera, 'when you've seen one, you've seen them all.'

'I know, but this one's eating my crisps and winkin' at me!!'

Freaky Villas

My Life, Loves and Not Tonight Headaches
**by Marlene Coke, Paymate of the Year, Panty
House Pet and Page Three Scrubber
As told to Reg Letch, *Daily Gutter* Ace Reporter.**

Quick Poke Coke
I was born simple Marlene Coke. My father was a simple
country vicar. We lived simply in the country. As a
growing girl I looked around me and saw all Nature at it.
The sheep were doing it, the hedgehogs were doing it,
the birds were doing it, the rabbits were doing it, I was
doing it too, but I was the only one charging for doing it.
As he watched me playing with my little friends behind
the shed where he wrote his sermons and entertained his
choirboys, little did my father know that the little girl
who was doing it for sherbet and Dinky toys would one
day do it for real Morris Minors, and that princes would
eat sherbet from my navel and drink stale beer from my
Wellington boot.

Convent Girl Has Gardener
When I was twelve I went to the convent school of St
Scrofulus set in the lovely Salford countryside, and it was
there I met Old Ben the gardener, who was to be my

lover for three years until his pension ran out. His horny hands would rip the flimsy school uniform off my young body and, as he thrust money into my piggy bank, we would fall backwards over the piles of old copies of *Health and Efficiency* in the potting shed, my bra tangled in the wires of his hearing aid. By the time I was fourteen I had the body of a fully grown woman and the mind of an eighty-year-old merchant banker. I could take them as fast as you could throw them under me and, at the height of passion, would wrap my legs around their backs to work out the VAT on my toes.

Jet Set Dolly Bird in Muck Jiggers' Bed

By the time I was seventeen I'd won my first beauty contest and was Miss Gland, Lights, Liver and Blood, 1974, voted first in the Salford Abattoir Beauty Queen contest. My father was not far away in Strangeways doing time for bumping into a choirboy who had bent down to tie his shoelaces.

It was at the Salford Abattoir that I met Huge Offener, the owner of *Payboy* magazine. He had everything a woman wants and it was all in Swiss banks.

'With tits like those you should be on the centre spread,' he chortled wittily, as we tucked into a dinner of cow's udder and champagne after the contest. 'I'm gonna make you a household name,' he said, stuffing tenners into the sack I had accidently dropped at his feet. I knew he was a man of the world as he threw me into his private tram and flew me off to his love nest in Eccles.

'If only the girls in Macfisheries could see me now,' I thought to myself, as I lay on his circular ratskin-covered love-bed with a toll-gate between my knees.

Pencil Sharpeners in the Bath and Blue Movies

Huge was an insatiable lover. At times my till got red-

30

hot and some nights I'd have to get up three or four times to oil my drawers. In the end I had to get a Barclaycard machine. But we tired of each other. He grew inattentive to me and forgot the little things that a girl likes her man to do, like shouting out the Dow Jones Index at his crisis and murmuring stock reports into her ear.

When I said I wanted a family he bought me one but they were Greeks and I didn't understand them and had to have them put down.

Huge was a very kinky lover too. He used lots of aphrodisiacs. Before a night of love he would swallow huge amounts of chocolate money and together we would sniff twenty-pound notes till our heads spun. He was into blue movies as well and used to show hard-core porn films of bankers doing things to piggy banks and businessmen leaping off buildings in the great crash.

Sex Oil and Marzipan

At the height of our passionate embraces he would scream filth at me like 'Marx and Lenin', 'Nationalization', and 'Money can't buy everything'. I don't know where he got his filthy ideas from. Afterwards he always felt very guilty. One of the kinkiest things he wanted me to do was dress up as a social worker, but I refused. I was kinky – but that was going too far. He loved to dress me up in bank statements made from marzipan and he would eat them from my body.

Worst of all was the oil. Huge loved to rub me all over with a special sex oil he had made exclusively for himself from rendered-down bankruptcy orders. He would massage me with it for hours muttering, 'Keynes, Keynes . . . your breasts, your breasts.' I often had to point out that it was my knees he was massaging because his Citizen Kane mask used to slip down over his eyes. Once he put so much oil on me that I shot out of his arms and through the hotel bedroom door, and had to be prised out from behind a radiator with a pair of snail tongs, a hatpin, and a promise of a new yacht.

Huge was my first real lover, before him I'd had affairs – thousands of them – but Huge was the only one who'd opened a dollar trading account with me. Things like that mean a lot to a girl.

Next Week:
I MAKE LOVE TO AN EXTRA-TERRESTIAL. . . . GOING MUFF-DIVING WITH HANS AND LOTTEE . . . all in your fabulous *Daily Gutter.* **. . .**

Freaky Villas

Was a one-night gig in London Town,
The band had all gone home.
I was packin' my guitar,
Thought I was alone.
Then I saw her standing
In the candle-light.
She smoothed out her rubber dress
And squeezed me with her eyes.

Chorus: Come to Freaky Villas,
You're gonna have some fun.
Bring your leather and your chains,
You'll be glad you come.

She said, 'Come home with me, young man,
Rest your weary head.'
Like Moses in reverse,
Into bondage I was led.
Her flat was full of Kenwood Chefs,
Pneumatic drills and things;
Clockwork marrows and false noses
Hanging up on strings.

She dressed up as a welder,
And dressed me as a cowboy.
Led me to the water bed
And shouted, 'Saddle up, boy!!!'
'I've never had a rowing boat!'
Were the last words that I said,
'Cos the spurs on my cowboy boots
Popped the water bed!

The water shot off everywhere,
Cascaded out the door,
And freaks of every shape and size
Got washed off every floor.
A bloke in bed with a camel
Hit the wall with a hell of a bump,
Broke his teeth and glasses
Gave the camel another hump.

A bloke surfed out on an ironing board,
Talking to his right hand.
Fred Astaire was rogering Ginger
To the music of the band.
Andy Pandy and Looby Loo
In the streets were swimmin',
And sixteen bishops paddled out
On blow-up rubber women.

The river police came paddling up
In a bath with flashing lights,
The inspector was dressed as a can-can girl
With ladders in his tights.
They formed a circle round us,
Said, "'Ello, 'ello, 'ello,
We've got a right lot 'ere, lads,
'It 'em wiv your dildos.'

So if you go to London Town
And find yourselves alone,
Don't go with those young Cockney
   girls
That want to take you home.
If you see a girl in a polythene bag,
Sink plungers on her knee
And skin-tight rubber braces,
Don't go, it might be me.

Freaky Villas

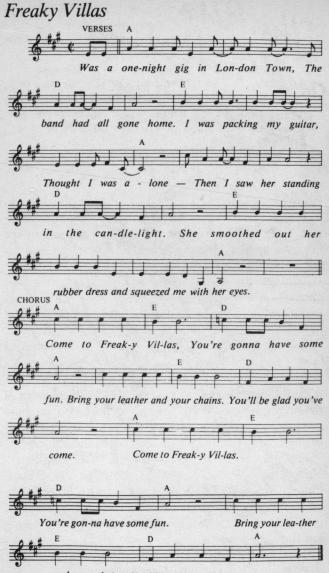

VERSES

Was a one-night gig in Lon-don Town, The band had all gone home. I was packing my guitar, Thought I was a-lone — Then I saw her standing in the can-dle-light. She smoothed out her rubber dress and squeezed me with her eyes.

CHORUS

Come to Freak-y Vil-las, You're gonna have some fun. Bring your leather and your chains. You'll be glad you've come. Come to Freak-y Vil-las.

You're gon-na have some fun. Bring your lea-ther and your chains. You'll be glad you've come.

The Rise and Fall of my Brother Jim

It's a wet November evening. Wind blows birds backwards over the Pennines. The standing stones on Blackstone Edge are lying down. Heathcliff is at home by the fire playing Scrabble. Captain Oates has changed his mind about going out.

Through the wet, howling hell of this night a light appears on a lonely moorland road. The light becomes two. The two lights make a noise, a growling noise. Out of the mist of Kinder Scout appears a Ford Thames van. A very old Ford Thames van, such a van as Caesar might have used to cross the Rubicon. It is a red van, going very slowly, uphill. Three of the spark plugs are wet. It is firing on one cylinder. It struggles to within ten yards of the summit. Then the faint life within the carbonized and cracked heart of the beast dies and for a while all is still as the bald tyres slowly kiss the road to a standstill.

From inside the van five voices cry, 'Oh no!', 'Shit!', 'All out!' and 'Here we bloody go again!' in various keys. Four of the voices get out complete with bodies. The bodies line up at the back of the van and begin pushing it painfully upwards through the chilling rain shouting encouragement to the driver.

'Let the handbrake off, you dozy bugger!'

'Come on, prattface! Get it out of gear.'

'Come on, play the white man . . . get your foot off the bleedin' brake!'

On the side of the van painted in very rough letters is the awe-inspiring legend, RIKKI AND THE RENEGADES.

A sheep runs in the road. The driver brakes hard. Four wet heads bang on the van's back door. One nose begins to bleed. The sheep is frightened. The sheep does what all sheep do when they are frightened and leaves half a hundredweight of sheep turds on the road.

'What the bloody hell did you stop for?'

'Oh fug, be dodes pleedink!'

'You pratt!'

'You dozy bugger!'

From the front comes the reply, 'It was only a sheep for God's sake! Come on! Get pushing or we'll be late for the gig!!'

Four wet bodies carry on pushing, shouting:

'I never wanted to be a rock and roll star anyway!'

'Neider did I!'

'What price daddy's yacht now?'

'I wish I was back in the bloody factory cannin' lettuce.'

They near the summit. One of the pushers slips on the heap of sheep turds and falls in the wet road. The other three laugh. He doesn't. The van, gathering momentum, begins to roll down the hill. They chase it and jump in. Four wet bodies and a dry one.

'You never bleedin' push!'

'I'm the driver.'

'What time we got to be there?'

'Seven o'clock.'

'Stroll od, we'll dever do id!'

'Who are we on with?'

'Some band called The Hollies and another band called Herman's Hermits.'

'I bet they're both crap.'

'Where we playing?'

'Leek Town Hall.'

'Bloody Nora!'

'Stroll od!'

'Oh shit, not Leek again . . . Deadsville! There's more life in Co-Op bacon!'

'The car park'll be full of farm tractors again.'

'Pig muck on the dance floor off all the boots.'

Off down the hill went the Ford Thames van, spluttering into life, smelling of wet clothes, sheep muck and feet, laboriously spraying the Derbyshire air with foul language.

I know. I was one of those Renegades.

Strange But True

If an atom bomb destroyed the centre of Birmingham the cheers would be heard 233 miles away.

The Rise and Fall of my Brother Jim

I had a brother Jim, he was a singer in a rock and roll band.
In a red Ford Thames he travelled all over the land.
Had all the girls eatin' right out of his hand,
Had 'em on a mattress lyin' in the back of the van.

Chorus
He was a rock and roll singer, knew just how to go.
In his silver lamé clogs he always stole the show.

He was livin' on Wimpys, sleepin' on the motorway,
Singin' all night, travellin' all through the day.
His pictures appeared in the *Sketch* and the *Daily Mail*.
For fighting in Cleckheaton he spent three nights in jail.

Got boozed on stage and smashed up the drummer's kit,
Trousers so tight every time he moved they split,
Then he'd grab a girl and take her off to the van,
He lost four front teeth to the boot of one bird's old man.

Then one night in Hartlepool
Their eyes met across a crowded room.
She was a quite pissed typist from a typing pool,
In Hartlepool, she was no fool,
Her eyes were like the dark night sky
That rides above the motorway.
And with a laugh and a flash of her smiling eyes . . .
She took his mind away . . .
From the band . . . travellin' the land . . . rock and roll man
Ford Thames van . . .

Then every other week we were up round Hartlepool
Singin' 'Who hung the Monkey?' and 'Bye Bye, Daddy Cool'.
A bun in the oven and church bells began to sing,
He sold the Ford Thames van to buy a wedding ring.

See him now in the boozer on a Friday night
In his long drape jacket and his trousers oh so tight.
He feeds the juke box and be-bop-a-lullas away
Till his wife comes round to drag him back home again.

Now he works in a factory makin' ashtrays for motor bikes,
Many a time he thinks back to the old nights
When he was a singer singin' in a rock and roll band,
Carrying a harem in the back of a Ford Thames van.

The Rise and Fall of my Brother Jim

Bright Rock and Roll

I had a bro-ther Jim, he was a sin-ger in a rock and roll band.

In a red Ford Thames he tra-velled all ov-er the land.

Had all the girls eat-in' right out of his hand,

Had 'em on a matt-ress

ly-in' in the back of the van. –   *He was a*

CHORUS

rock and roll sin-ger. Knew just how to go —   *In his*

sil-ver la-mé clogs he al-ways stole the show.

Comrade Olga

If the right-wing scaremongers in the country are correct and the sky is about to grow dark with parachuting Ivans, while the cellar grids of Chinese takeaways spring open to pour forth legions of Maoist troops, and the Pudsey Branch of the Budgie-Bung Carvers' and Wick-Knitters' Guild is found to be a Trotskyite cell, then I think it's probably time that I started writing Russian songs, particularly now that we have the new public office of Art Critic and Spy by Royal Appointment. Even more fascinating is the thought that if Britain does become one of the countries in the West European Soviet bloc, then my own trade would be collectivized as fast as that of any platelayer, grinder or surgical truss designer.

Report of the 14th Commune Comedians' Collective, Oswaldtwhistle Branch, November Meeting

Chairman Brother Ron 'he's the boy' Clarke:

'Comrade comics. After reading the minutes of the last meeting, Brother Chairman wishes to inform you that the Committee has proposed the following business for discussion on tonight's agenda:

1. The recent failure of some of our members to observe the guidelines laid down in the *Codebook of Jokes, Gags and One-Liners* for use by performing artistes in the Soviet Western bloc.

2. The second five-year plan for improving output in the world of entertainment including pre-breakfast comedy shows for nightshift workers in Luton and dinner-time Stripperama Bingo for the workers in the Wolverhampton rag-reprocessing plant.

3. The report of the Soviet International Commission on comedy led by comrades Bygraves, Tarbuck and Sykes, together with the amendments tabled by the Northern Committee on Decentralization chaired by Comrades Manning and Dawson. I now declare the meeting open and call on Jimmy "the Lad" Wigan to read the report.'

Comrade Wigan then read the report.

'Brothers and Comrades. There have been several serious cases of alternative thinking in the last few months and many of our comrade comics have been found to be in the pay of the running dogs of Imperialism and have been liquidated or have asked for political asylum in Dublin. Comrade "Laughing Legs" Lonnigan, comedian and eccentric dancer, was paid off again after only seven minutes of his act at the Colchester Carburettor and Spam Works Social Club and has been sentenced by the committee to four weeks' hard labour at Stockton Coke Retort and Washhouses Leisure Centre as opening act to Enrico and His Whistling Ferrets.' (Mutters of 'Oh God!', 'That's a bit strong!', 'Poor bastard!', etc.)

'Comrade "Happy Lungs" Cassidy, the balloon sculpture and comedy act, did so badly at the Leeds and Chapeltown Embalmers' and Mortuary Attendants' Benefit Smokers' Night that he's been sentenced to a month at the Talk of the Town, Echelfechan, and two months at Caesar's Palace, Bacup, the sentences to run concurrently. His agent is now working as a teabag dryer for British Soviet Rail.' (Cries of 'Quite right', 'Serves him right', etc.)

'Comrades Dino Swift and Roland Sonne who recently developed their own particular branch of satirical political comedy are retiring from show business. Their widows are prepared to sell their props and will be putting adverts in *The Stage*.

'Lastly, Comrade Eric "Mr Showbiz" Diamonds and his ventriloquist dummy Woody have been in trouble again for criticizing Comrades Grade and Delfont, our glorious leaders. Comrade Diamonds claims that it was the dummy that said it not him, so we've called in Rentokil to see to the dummy.'

Strange But True

In 1972 thieves broke into Manchester docks and stole £3000 worth of bananas under the closed eyes of a sleeping nightwatchman. Police are looking for a gang of quiet elephants.

Comrade Olga

Comrade Olga can be Volga
When she wants to be,
This pretty miss kissed Ivanovitch
In the tractor factory,
She put her hand inside his Bolsheviks
And tickled Ivan's balalaikas.

Chorus
Comrade Olga, get your Trotskys off.
Down with the bourgeoisie!
Comrade Olga, get your Trotskys off,
Olga, be Volga with me!

Comrade Olga she was married
To Boris Pizdov,
He was not happy that his Olga
Liked to Trotsky off,
And since Boris had muscles in his roubles
Ivan Ivanovitch kept his balalaikas to himself.

Comrade Olga said to Ivan,
'My Boris works nights.
Do you not thinksy that a drinksky
At my flatsky would be nice?
It's not risky, I've some whisky and some ice,
So let's get shmasky and have a bashky tonight.'

So Comrade Olga and her Ivan
Got drunk as newtskies.
She said, 'I'm hotsky to Trotsky!'
Threw off her clothskys and bootskys,
And as the moonlight flitted across her minarets,
The fluff all blew off Ivan's balalaikas.

Just thensky came a knocksky
At the front doorbellsky,
Ivan had tremlins in his Kremlins,
Whispered, 'Bloody hellsky!'
And, as Boris came crashing through the doorsky,
Under the bedsky Ivanovitch did go.

Now when Boris saw his Olga
In the nudsky stood,
He offsky threwsky allsky clothsky
As fasky asky could,
And to the bedsky they did gosky
As Ivansky lay with his headsky in the posky.

Now poor Ivansky has his nosky stuckovitch
In the springsky,
Every bumpsky of the bedsky
Made the posky ringsky,
And as the bedsky got fastasky so did his headsky,
Till it sounded like the Moscow fire alarmsky.

'There's a redsky under the bedsky!'
Boris loudly cried.
'I am Pizdov!'
'I don't like it either,' Ivanovitch replied.
But just thensky insky came the fire brigadesky
And soaked everybodsky with their hoseky pipeskies.

Oh, to the salt mines Boris and Ivansky
They were sentovitch.
For a false alarmsky fourteen yearsky,
Oh sonofabitch!
But Olga does not give a Vladivistok,
'Cos every nightsky she rattles the posky,
And to her flat the fire brigade gosky
And she blows the fluff off all their balalaikas!

Comrade Olga

VERSES 1,2,3
Colla voce Fm

Com-rade Ol-ga — can be Vol-ga When she wants to be This pretty miss kissed Iv-an-o-vitch in the tractor fac-tor-y. — She put her hand in-side his Bol-she--viks, and tick-led Iv-an's - ba-la-lai-kas, Oh -

CHORUS *a tempo*

Com-rade Ol-ga, get your Trotskys off. Down with the bour-geois -ie, oi, oi, oi, Com-rade Ol-ga get your Trot-skys off.

D.C. twice for verses 2 & 3

1. Ol-ga be Vol-ga with me I, I, I.

2. me, oi, oi,

St George Doesn't Live Here Any More

Legend has it that after the last battle of the Knights of the Round Table Arthur sailed across the lake to Avalon. Other legends say that he lies with his knights buried in the heart of a hill somewhere in England and that outside the hall where the King lies sleeping, out on the windy hillside, is a golden horn that will be found again and sounded when England is in grave peril. Then Arthur and Merlin and the Knights of the Round Table will ride out from under the hill to Her aid.

It is a grey November Saturday morning in 1983. The drizzle is falling over Littlehampton New Town, a megopolis of some 900,000 souls, principal manufactory, CYBERNETIC INTERNATIONAL, principal manufactures: Ivansky Soya Bean Caviar Substitute, Joocey Loocey Bubble Gum, Goggle'n Guzzle Instant TV Dinners and the Cluckey Luckey Aerosol Omelette Can.

The old village of Littlehampton-on-the-Mire, saved by a plethora of preservation orders, nestles between the strutting columns of the M6/M7/M8/M1/M4/M62 Maggie Thatcher Way-Interlink-Feeder-Bypass-Cat's-Cradle-Junction. The Norman Tower of Littleham

Church, where Wat Tyler strung up the head of the Lord of the Manor, is just fouteeen inches from the arch of the flyover, where migrating Euro Juggernauts with their six trailers smash on towards the Cross Channel Bridge, answering the call in the nation's pulse for more of everything. Where now are your caravanserai, your stately triremes, your barques fresh laden from lands of spice and mystery? Gone and faded away; instead the Juggernauts of Billy Blake, Albion Roadhaulage Co. are en route for Köln to pick up 3000 tons of *Bratwurst* for Sainsbury's, Wigan.

Over Littlehampton New Town the drizzle still falls. It falls on the Rollerama Super Disco, the Hyperdrome Dance Baths and the 13,000-seater Mississippi Fried Pizzarama and Spaghetti Palace, where an army of bored waitresses in Neapolitan dustbin ladies' costume stand round chewing in the same rhythm and serving lukewarm stewed coffee substitute and gut-strangulating stodge to the overweight coronary-bound populace of Littlehampton, where dandruff, haemorrhoids, acne and ulcers are a way of life.

This Saturday morning, the drizzle falls wearily on the cars that pull off the by-pass in their thousands, following the clusters of arrows and flashing signals that take them from the Keith Joseph Estate and the Blessed St John Stevas Underground Tower Block to the multi-storey car park shopping precinct centre at the heart of Littlehampton.

Mr and Mrs Wart and their son Bede drive up the ramp towards the car park of the biggest macro-market in Western Europe. As ever, it is almost full, and everywhere, dentured, paunchy parents, whose only exercise is Armchair Televideo Squash are loading the week's convenience foods into the boots of their family saloons.

The Warts, unable to find a space at the lower levels,

drive, cursing and squabbling, on to the roof level and find, as though by fate, the last available space. In the centre of the roof is a tree, a small, weak, almost dead tree. It was put there by the Town Clerk, the planners and the architect, planted with a silver gilt spade to commemorate the mighty forest that once stood below the concrete steppes of Littlehampton New Town.

Little Bede Wart runs to the tree.

'Look, mam, look, dad! A big wooden flower!!!'

'Don't be silly, Bede – that's a tree.'

'A tree – flip me! I seen one of them in a video comic once – flip me!'

'Don't you go touchin' that soil – I didn't pay good money for them clothes for you to go touchin' no soil!'

But it is too late. Before she can stop him, Bede has climbed the retaining wall and is stood on the wet earth dumped by the crane on the day the roof was completed. The soil had come from Littlehampton Barrow before it disappeared under the Newtown Arndale Centre.

Something gleams at little Bede's feet.

'Look, mam, dad, I found somethin'!'

'You put that down, it's dirty.'

''Ere, son – let's look – it's an 'orn or somefink.'

'I bet it's worth a lot of money, eh, dad, eh?'

'Could be, son – could be. We'll take it down the antique shop after we've had a Spamburger – now come on or we'll be late for Shoppy Bingorama.'

They set off, walking towards the supermarket stairs. Little Bede Wart washes the horn out in a puddle and shakes it dry. The moving stairs and lift aren't working as usual so they begin to walk down the dark concrete stairwell that smells of wet and dogs. On the aerosoled stairway little Bede puts the horn to his lips. Along the spirals of the precast towers the horn's note sings out loud and clear; out over the concrete wastes, it re-echoes, shattering the lowering skies that lean down on the reinforced grey acres. The clear shrill clarion sails out across the heavens.

'You little bleeder (crack, wallop).'

'Ouch, mam!'

'You'll get bleedin' germs from that (crack, wallop)! There's dog kak in that soil (wallop, crack).'

A creaking could be heard in the dark hall below the hill. Old leather moved. Breastplate brushed against guidon, chain mail stretched and rubbed against linen for the first time in a millennium. A sword clashed against the bare, black jut of rock and shattered the dark. The sleeping knights were a-slumber no more. Their king raised his mighty arms and stretched out yawning, flexing his muscles as he had done before drawing the sword from the stone all those many mornings ago.

'My knights, the horn has called. The last battle of all will be met.' His voice boomed in the darkness. 'England is in peril, Knights of the Round Table. Though we should fall we will not fail in this, the last Great Quest.'

The knights stood ready, their hands on their swords, waiting. A small page boy brought from out of the gloom a snow-white horse, Arthur's horse; behind, obediently came the mounts of his faithful knights. By the king stood the old wizard Merlin in a dark cloak, carrying a wondrous wand. Arthur and the knights mounted.

'Merlin, speak the words for Albion,' Arthur commanded.

Merlin raised his arms and in a voice that thrilled all the company called on the hill to open:

> *'Eli kazaar melthidadon*
> *Eloim galadrin melthidadon*
> *Galadri galadri Excalibur!*
> *Eli kazar morg Albion!'*

With a flash of lightning and a crack of thunder the doors of the Great Barrow swung open and King Arthur and the knights of the Round Table rode out on their white steeds, leaping over the frozen TV dinner counter, demolishing mountains of instant potato tins and Doggie Chocs, as open-mouthed shoppers stared at the men on horseback pouring through the gaping hole in Sainsbury's back wall.

Strange But True

Thieves broke into London Docks last month and stole a container-load of forty tons of hazelnuts. Police are looking for a gang of squirrels with hernias and heavy goods licences.

St George Doesn't Live Here Any More

The old school team are all bowled out,
In the Quad no voices shout,
St George is in the sauna and the girls are rubbing him down,
John Bull is down in old Soho
Watching Linda Lovelace blow
A horn that good old Gabriel would have been proud to own.

Chorus
So light the lamp and shut the door!
Tea and stickies, half-past four.
St George doesn't live here anymore!

Camelot has gone to pot,
They've sold it as a development plot,
Over Arthur and his knights is another Centre Point.
Peter Pan and Tigger and Poo
Are in the nursery sniffiing glue,
While Noddy's popping bennies and Big Ears rolls a joint.

No longer do the branches stir
Across the moon at Grantchester,
And beneath the dreaming spires they've hatched another
    neutron bomb.
Tom Brown's in Borstal, he's been done.
Across the world the twilight sun has set.
The Empire's in the dark and the lights won't go back on.

Sherlock Holmes and Dan Dare
Are very big in stocks and shares,
And are very, very busy selling England by the pound.
And with the minimum of malice
Christopher Robin has burgled the Palace,
Alice is on the game and Knightsbridge is her round.

St. George Doesn't Live Here Any More

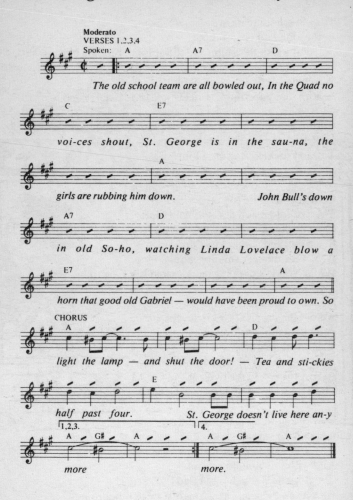

Moderato
VERSES 1,2,3,4
Spoken:

The old school team are all bowled out, In the Quad no voi-ces shout, St. George is in the sau-na, the girls are rubbing him down. John Bull's down in old So-ho, watching Linda Lovelace blow a horn that good old Gabriel — would have been proud to own. So

CHORUS

light the lamp — and shut the door! — Tea and sti-ckies half past four. St. George doesn't live here an-y more

more.

The Hattersley Lament

Hattersley is a Manchester Corporation-built housing estate, half on the edge of the Pennines and half on the cap-neb side of Cheshire. I used to work on the buses in Manchester, and on a Friday and Saturday night the people of Hattersley used to go in droves into Manchester for a night out, because the social life on the housing estate made Mars look like Las Vegas. On the way back from Manchester, the last bus would be jammed, reeking of ale and doom and driven by a driver who knew it was his last trip and took it round corners at such an angle that I used to walk along the windows to collect the fares. Then someone would start singing the verse about Hattersley and soon the whole bus would be singing like Christians going to the lions, the verses ringing on and on, broken only by the sound of the occasional woman hitting her husband with a Chinese takeaway or somebody who'd had too much ale throwing it all back up over the top of the stairwell.

I've always been fascinated with what authorities do to people when they knock down their towns and houses, reorganize them and package them off into manageable estates that nearly always turn into vandalized concrete wildernesses. For my sins I once worked on the infamous Manchester Corporation Hulme Development as a labourer one summer. We navvies knew we were building slums, the sub-contractors knew we were building slums, it seemed that everybody knew we were building slums but nobody did anything about it. Strange.

Strange But True

Anthropologists in East Africa announced the discovery of a primitive tribe who have made contact with the white man for the first time. They are called the Oominhakas and although they have normal-sized bodies their legs are a mere thirteen inches long. They inhabit the arid crater regions of Mganga where the only vegetations is a covering of dense stinging nettles that grow to an average height of thirteen and a half inches. The name of the tribe translated means 'The short-legged, running, jumping and shouting people whose eyes water a lot'.

The Curse of Morethanmy Jobsworth

A one-act one-scene play set in ancient Egypt at the time of the Pharoahs

ACT ONE – Scene One

Mrs Amenhotep is busy in the little kitchen of her terraced pyramid in Herakleopolis. The children have breakfasted and gone to school. On the radio the dulcet tones of Pterrie Woganezzar introduce a new record by the Pdooleys. Mrs Amenhotep brushes the hair back from her eyes and leans over the sink. There is a knock on the door; she opens it.

Councillor Angmeatop and his assistant Kwixtep are stood outside. They are holding theodolites, plans, sextants, bribes, etc.

COUNCILLOR ANGMEATOP	Good morning, madam, my name is Councillor Angemeatop and this is my assistant Kwixtep. We've come to knock your pyramid down.
MRS AMENHOTEP	Knock me pyramid down?
COUNCILLOR ANGMEATOP	Well, of course, you'll be allocated a new council pyramid on the new housing estate at Giza.
MRS AMENHOTEP	Giza! I don't want to move all the way to Giza in one of them multi-storey pyramids near that bloomin' great Sphinx; there's no buses, no shops, no pubs, nowhere for the kids to play. The lifts are never working and the place is filthy – covered in all them aerosol graffiti like 'Nefertiti does it for Osiris' and

'Memphis Mods rool OK?' And what about me mother in Luxor? How am I going to afford the chariot fare to manage to get over and see her?

KWIXTEP   But there's Old People's Homes.

MRS AMENHOTEP   She won't go in one of them – she likes her own little pyramid – got it all nice she has with her own little things.

COUNCILLOR   But you see there's been a com-
ANGMEATOP   pulsory purchase order and the whole area's being cleared to make way for the Memphis to Thebes Clearway.

MRS AMENHOTEP   You're all the same, you lot. You draw up your plans and come along and just knock things down and move people about. Who do you think you are, eh? What about the kids? Where are they going to play with all them eight-wheeled oxen carts trundling past? And what about all them foreigners down there, them Israelites? Not safe out, it isn't, with all them plagues of frogs and boils and all that. I'm not moving down there for nobody. And when are you going to do something about the smell from that frankincense factory? It's got my nerves bad. I've been under the doctor about it, I have. Your promises aren't worth the papyrus they're written on. (*She takes a theodolite and rams it down Kwixtep's throat. Kwixtep dies.*)

COUNCILLOR ANGMEATOP: Now, love, it's no use blamin' us. We're only doing our job. Sithee, by 'eck. It's more than our job's worth not to do what we're told. We're just acting on orders; the law's the law, and where would we all be if we went round doing just what we felt like, eh? Answer me that.

Lights fade and the curtain falls on the Valley of the Kings New Town.

The Hattersley Lament

Our cat's no hair on, no hair on, no hair on,
Our cat's no hair on, 'e as to wear a wig.
If you don't believe me, believe me, believe me,
If you don't believe me, then come and 'ave a look.

I've got a gumboil, a pimple, a bellyache,
I've got a gumboil, a pimple on me bum.
If you don't believe me, believe me, believe me.
If you don't believe me, then come and 'ave a look.

Chorus
Oh dear what can the matter be,
Some silly bugger 'as sent us to 'Attersley,
We've bin up 'Attersley three weeks on Saturday,
Ee, 'ow I wish you was 'ere.

From our toilet in the backyard,
You can sit and watch the stars,
One cold night while studying Jupiter,
I got frost bite on me Mars.

A fella came round from the Council,
'I've come to raise your rent,' he cried,
I said, 'By gum, lad, I'm glad to 'ear it,
I couldn't raise it if I tried.'

Butcher, butcher, give us a sheep's head,
Because we can't afford the best meat,
But, butcher, please don't pull its eyes out,
It's got to see us through next week.

My Uncle Jabez was fond of a stunt,
He went out one day with his coat back-to-front,
A blooming big truck came and knocked Jabez down,
He might have been saved but they turned his head round.

Chorus
Toora loo, toora lay,
For the best of Society lives down our way.

I called by for my fiancée, her name is Miss Brown,
She was 'aving a bath so she couldn't come down,
She said, 'I'll slip on something, luv, and be down in a tick,'
But she slipped on the soap and came down ruddy quick.

Well, I saw an old tramp, he was tattered and torn,
He was eating the grass on the front of our lawn,
He said, 'Ay, lad, can you give us a snack?'
I said, 'Yes, lad, the grass is longer around at the back.'

My Aunty Kitty she made a rice pud,
And when it was finished it tasted right good,
But she made it in't kettle and we couldn't get bugger out,
So we each took a turn to suck it out of the spout.

The Hattersley Lament

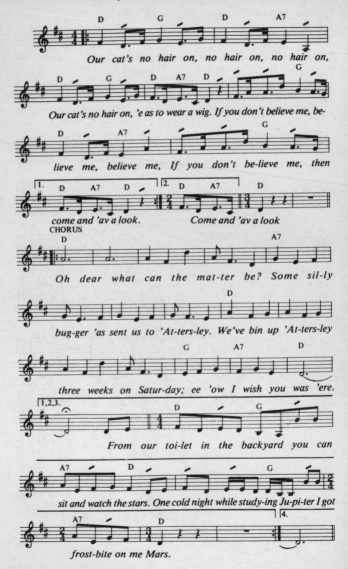

Our cat's no hair on, no hair on, no hair on,

Our cat's no hair on, 'e as to wear a wig. If you don't believe me, be-

lieve me, believe me, If you don't be-lieve me, then

1. come and 'av a look. 2. Come and 'av a look

CHORUS

Oh dear what can the mat-ter be? Some sil-ly

bug-ger 'as sent us to 'At-ters-ley. We've bin up 'At-ters-ley

three weeks on Satur-day; ee 'ow I wish you was 'ere.

1,2,3. From our toi-let in the backyard you can

sit and watch the stars. One cold night while study-ing Ju-pi-ter I got

4. frost-bite on me Mars.

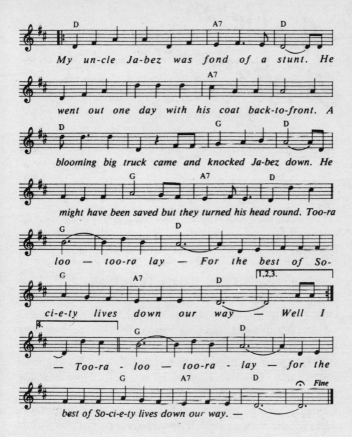

My un-cle Ja-bez was fond of a stunt. He
went out one day with his coat back-to-front. A
blooming big truck came and knocked Ja-bez down. He
might have been saved but they turned his head round. Too-ra
loo — too-ra lay — For the best of So-
ci-e-ty lives down our way — Well I
— Too-ra - loo — too-ra - lay — for the
best of So-ci-e-ty lives down our way. —

The German Clockwinder

'The German Clockwinder' is a traditional song about a horological gigolo based on a story by the Brothers Grimm, who also wrote the following fairytale:

The Princess, the Giant and the Three Pratts

There was once an old poor charcoal burner who lived in a hut in the heart of a dark forest at the foot of the Crystal Mountains. He had a son called Hans. Hans was a pratt who rode a motor bike and smoked in the outside toilet, so we can discount him immediately. He also had a son called Carl who had skin as fair as snow and lips like rubies because he stayed up all night abusing himself, bashing his bishop and playing the trumpet. So we'll ignore him as well. The youngest son of the woodcutter was called Eric. He was a simpleton with about as much common sense as a toad has feathers, but he didn't play the trumpet or with himself, so it's Eric, the youngest pratt, that we'll make the hero of our tale.

One day the old charcoal burner was searching for charcoal to burn with nothing in his poor leather satchel but a dry piece of black bread and a flask of spring water.

In the middle of the dark forest he came upon a house he had never seen before, a house made entirely of gingerbread, walnuts, pork scratchings, best steak and Blackpool rock, but as the old charcoal burner had no teeth he walked on into the dark forest.

After a year and a day (which meant he was now on overtime) he came upon an old man who was lying almost dead on the forest path with a thorn in his paw. The charcoal burner knelt down and gently took the thorn from the old man's paw, at the same time forcing the black bread and the water between the old man's teeth.

The old man opened one eye, choked a bit and revived. A moment later he sat on a stone and looked at the old charcoal burner with a twinkling nose, and shouted, 'I know you. You're the old charcoal burner that lives just over the other side of the forest near Gingerbread Flats.'

'How did you know that?' asked the old charcoal burner in amazement.

'I used to clean your windows,' said the old wizard, for that is what he really was. Window cleaning was just a front for his other activities such as reducing princes to toads, making princesses sleep on peas, and inventing itching powder and joke soap.

'You have three sons,' said the old wizard. 'Two of them are wastrels and ne'er-do-wells: the first will fall off his bike under a lorry, and the second will die when his pyjamas fall on him. The youngest son will make his fortune in the world and will look after you in your old age. Here, take this for your kindness.' And so saying, he handed the old man a torn piece of paper.

It was a cutting from the Personal Column of the *Black Forest Gazette*, which said:

'Princess's father offers hand of daughter in marriage to any charcoal burner's son who can rid kingdom of Gay Giant called Peasmold. Write Arnold King, Box 47.'

Also in the column was:

'Gay Giant, 42ft 6½in., wishes to meet similar. Interests music, needlework, theatre, ruining towns and eating people. Lonely, head in the clouds? Write Everard Peasmold, Box 48.' Days later, with a loaf, some cheese, a flask of spring water and a sword his father had made for him from some old Meccano, Eric set off to seek his fortune in the far-off kingdom of Box 47.

After a year and a day he saw before him the gates of the royal palace so he bought a ticket and went in. The palace was crowded with people, hanging from the balconies, milling in the courtyard and lounging in the corridors, for word had spread all over the kingdom of Box 47 that the charcoal burner's son was to fight the giant. A sudden silence came upon the multitude. Over the hills towards the palace strode the giant, kicking over pylons, and stamping on the Wimpy Bar.

'Hold, you great poofdah!' cried the charcoal burner's son, flashing his sword in the sunlight.

The princess looked down on him with love in her eyes, which was stupid because it was the first time she'd seen him – but then she was like that.

'Aroint thee, thou great queen!' shouted the brave charcoal burner's son.

'Straight bitch!' shouted the short-sighted giant as he smashed him into a pulp with his hand-made Gucci boots.

The moral of the story is: firstly, too much optimism is bad for you, and secondly; never take any notice of wizards stupid enough to get thorns in their paws. And more to the point. Don't take the mickey out of gay giants.

Strange But True

If the entire population of China jumped into the air at the same time and landed simultaneously the resulting shock would send the earth into orbit round Pluto. This would cause the melting of the polar ice caps and a mammoth seaweed harvest in the Andes while the Oasis at Rotherham would become the meeting place for nomadic herdsmen wandering across the West Yorkshire Dustbowl. In the light of this terrible knowledge a top-secret delegation left for Peking yesterday to have talks on the strategic limitation of jumping tests and the immediate cessation of underground jumping tests.

The German Clockwinder

Well, a German clockwinder to Manchester came,
Benjamin Von Gherkins was the old German's name,
All up our street with his little brass bell,
'Clocks for to wind,' this old German would yell.

Chorus
I toodle um I toodle um I toodle um I ay,
I toodle um I toodle um in the old-fashioned way,
I toodle um I toodle um I toodle um I ay,
Well, I wind 'em by night and I mend 'em by day.

Now this old German was the ladies' delight,
And he often went to them by day and by night,
Some went too fast like and others went too slow,
But nine out of ten he could make 'em all go.

Now he met a young woman in Stevenson Square,
She said that her clock was in need of repair,
She took him upstairs and he followed with delight,
And in less than ten minutes he'd set her clock right.

Now while they was busy at what they was at,
All of a sudink there came a rat tat,
In came her hubby who got such a shock,
When he saw that old German winding up his wife's clock.

Now 'er clock it were bent and knocked out of repair,
And that poor old German he got such a scare,
That never oh never for the rest of his life,
Will he wind up the clock of another man's wife.

The German Clockwinder

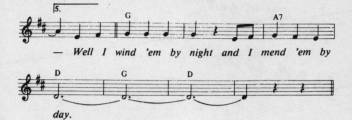

— *Well I wind 'em by night and I mend 'em by*

day.

The Keyhole in the Door

Oh, they all had left the parlour a quarter after nine,
By lucky chance of fortune, lads, her room was next to mine,
For first like brave Columbus, her regions to explore,
I took up my position by the keyhole in the door.

Oh, the keyhole in the door,
Oh, the keyhole in the door,
I took up my position by the keyhole in the door.

Now this maiden first proceeded to take off her pretty dress,
Likewise her undergarments, lads, she'd twenty, more or less,
To tell the truth sincerely she had at least a score,
But I couldn't count them all like, through the keyhole in the
    door.

Through the keyhole in the door,
Through the keyhole in the door,
I couldn't count them all like, through the keyhole in the door.

Now she sat down on the sofa, with such a graceful ease,
And threw her pretty petticoat an inch above her knees,
A pair of sky-blue garters upon her thighs she wore,
By gum, she did look charming through the keyhole in the
    door.

Through the keyhole in the door,
Through the keyhole in the door,
By gum, she did look charming through the keyhole in the
door.

Now she ran up to the fire, her pretty form to warm,
With nothing but her shimmy on to hide her pretty form,
Oh, pray take off that shimmy, luv, I ask for nothing more,
By gum, I saw her do it through the keyhole in the door.

Through the keyhole in the door,
Through the keyhole in the door,
By gum, I saw her do it through the keyhole in the door.

Now this maiden then proceeded to get into her bed,
But first she blew the candle out and darkness reigned instead,
The hair it stood up on my neck like bristles in the boar,
By gum, I felt like jumping through the keyhole in the door.

Through the keyhole in the door,
Through the keyhole in the door,
By gum, I felt like jumping through the keyhole in the door.

So I went down to the parlour, me little joke to share,
And a great big strappin' likely lad I found standing there.
When I told him of me little joke he gave a terrible roar,
I'd been lookin' at his misses through the keyhole in the door.

Well, the tables crashed around me as I fell on me back,
And the landlord's aspidistra it gave me such a crack.
When I woke up in the mornin' me body was black and sore,
I felt as though he'd stuffed me through the keyhole in the
door.

The Keyhole in the Door

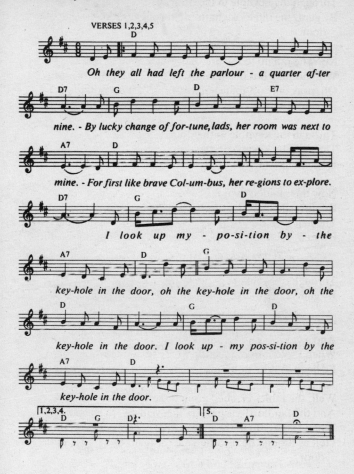

The Drunken Tackler

The tackler came home rolling drunk, as drunk as a lad could
    be,
Saw a bike outside the door where his bike ought to be,
And he said, 'Ey up, my beautiful wife, my darling wife,' said
    he,
'Whose is that bike outside the door where my owd bike should
    be?'
'Oh, you owd fool, you blind fool, you silly owd bugger,' said
    she,
'That's a lovely mangle that me mother sent to me.'
'Well, it's many a mile I travelled from Bowton up to Shaw
But pedals on a mangle I never saw before.'

He saw a cap inside the hall.
'That's a lovely pudding bowl my mother sent to me.'
'A sweat band on a pudding bowl I never saw before.'

He saw a clog beneath the bed.
'That's a lovely chamber po my mother sent to me.'
'Irons on a chamber po I never saw before.'

He saw a leg inside the bed.
'That's a lovely yard prop that me mother sent to me.'
'Bunions on a yard prop I never saw before.'

He saw a head upon the bed.
'That's a lovely cabbage my mother sent to me.'
'Glasses on a cabbage I never saw before.'

A thing in his wife's hand.
'That's a lovely rolling pin my mother sent to me.'
'Nutmegs on a rolling pin I never saw before.'

Strange But True

The insectiverous four-fingered sloth mates once every twelve years. The mating takes from three to four months and results in the male sloth having to take out a mortgage on a terraced house in Guatemala while he waits.

The Drunken Tackler

VERSES

The tack-ler came home rol-ling drunk, as drunk as a lad could be. Saw a bike out-side the door where his bike ought to be, And he said, 'Ey up, my beau-ti-ful wife, my dar-ling wife,' said he. 'Whose is that bike out-side the door where my owd bike should be?' 'oh you owd fool, you blind fool, you sil-ly owd bug-ger,' said she, That's a love-ly mangle — that me mo-ther sent to me,' 'Well, it's ma-ny a mile I tra-velled, — from Bow-ton up to

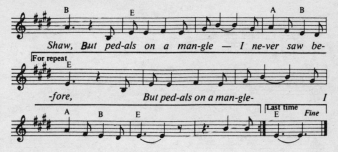

Shaw, But ped-als on a man-gle — I ne-ver saw be-fore, But ped-als on a man-gle- I ne-ver saw be-fore.'

Is That the Moon?

This song is the suit-ruining yodel of the Yates' Wine Lodge Light Ale Cavalry. They can be heard singing any Friday or Saturday night at the Mass Fall-Down Ceremony which takes place in commemoration of the discovery of Milk of Amnesia.

Further light has been thrown on this ceremony – which seems to date back many thousands of years – by the recent discovery of archaeological remains in the Olduvai Gorge, Blackburn, by Professor Leakey – probably best known for his discovery of Zinjanthropus Bosei, for which there is no known cure. His most recent discovery is that of the remains of an ape-like creature, half-humanoid in form, that could possibly be a link between man and the beast kingdom. Following on the discovery of Palaeolithic Man, Mesolithic Man and Neolithic Man, the new remains have been named Paralytic Man or 'homo horizontalis'.

Piecing together a large number of fragments of fossilized remains, Professor Leakey has come up with the theory that Paralytic Man was distinguished by a petrified liver, large abdomen and the ability to fall down without any notice. Anthropologists in England, working in close conjunction with the Coke Marketing

Board, have propounded a theory that, far from the humanoid Paralytic Man being extinct, it is in fact thriving within the present day social strata, having retained many of the characteristics that accrued to it during its spelaeological period.

Paralytic Man is known to travel in nomadic circles to worship at sacred wells that are dedicated to the Gods Tetley, Boddington and Theakston, and even false gods like Bass Charrington and Watney Mann. The average day of the Paralytic Man consists of drinking sacred libations to the Gods at the sacred well and hunting the Logend. The Logend is a cork-and-wire-backed animal that can be found climbing up the walls of the sacred hostelries dedicated to the Gods Boddington, Theakston and Tetley. The Logend is killed by throwing small hunting spears into its back, shouting 'Doubletop Frof' and 'Jammy basser'.

After hunting the Logend and taking several libations of the water of the sacred well, Paralytic Man, uttering sacred incantations, then returns to the cave in the tribal double-decker chariots, where he tries to mate with the female of his species. The female of the species usually resists his advances but if she does not (that is, if she is impressed by the ritualistic getting-pants-off mating stumbling dance) Paralytic Man, or 'Homo non erectus' as he is also known, is usually unable to perform the high point of the ritual. It is believed that Paralytic Man now reproduces by binary fission, a form of reproduction employed also by amoebas and telescopes.

During the night Paralytic Man paces the floor of the cave warding off purple traffic wardens and characters from 'Crossroads', unable to sleep, communicating occasionally with the God Hughie, and with the arrival of dawn Paralytic Man drinks a libation to another of his Gods, Eno.

The walls of the cave are covered with paintings of fellow tribesmen, who dress in coloured hunting clothes and join with others from a rival tribe to hunt a small armadillo-type, leather-backed animal by kicking it through wooden trilithons into a net. The hunt is viewed by large numbers of Paralytic Men and is supervised by High Priests of the Druidic type called 'Refs'. Often, excitement at the killing of the 'Match', as the little animal is called, will become so high that calls for a human sacrifice to appease the Gods will be made and the cry 'Kill the Ref' will echo round the temple and votive bottles and paper banners stream out towards him.

After the killing of the 'Match', Paralytic Man retires again to sacred wells to drink more libations. The walls of part of the sacred well are set aside for the worship of the God, Shanks. Splashing the Shanks is an ancient ceremony dating back to pre-Christian days. The walls of the hall where Shanks Splashing takes place are covered with prayers hoping for success in the hunting of the 'Match' and naming hunters of great prowess. References can also be found to fertility rites and symbols and incantations to the God, Kilroy.

Although information about Paralytic Man is certainly lacking in any great quantity, one other piece of vital information is available. It is known that Paralytic Man hunts a fierce, heavy, green-backed, four-legged animal called the Snooker by lying on its back and knocking its balls into its pockets with a long stick.

Is That the Moon?

Late one night I was having some fun,
I woke up in the morning dressed as a nun!
Oh Lord! I ain't gonna drink,
Ain't gonna drink no more.
Goin' through the park with a pain in my head,
Fightin' the flowers for their beds.
Oh Lord! I ain't gonna drink,
Ain't gonna drink no more.

Chorus
Oh me, Oh my!
I feel so high
Is that the moon?
Or is it the sun up in the sky?
Hughie, Hughie, Hughie, Hughie,
Ruth, Ruth, Ruth.
Oh Lord! I ain't gonna drink,
Ain't gonna drink no more.

The kids had a Guy Fawkes under a lamp,
I give 'em my coat to keep it from the damp.
Oh Lord! I ain't gonna drink,
Ain't gonna drink no more.
Bought a pigeon in a pub,
That damn bird was no damn good.
A homing pigeon it was called,
It never took me home at all.

Late one night I'd had a few jars
Climbed in the cage with the budgerigar
Oh Lord! I ain't gonna drink,
Ain't gonna drink no more.
That old budgie thought it was a game;
Every time I stood up, he knocked me down again.
Oh Lord! I ain't gonna drink,
Ain't gonna drink no more.

One night I'd had too much to drink,
Woke up sleeping in the sink.
Dreamt I'd eaten an old stale bun
Woke up . . . the soap and the flannel were gone.
Met a drunk in Blackpool town,
Sold him the Tower for a couple of pound,
You should have heard him curse and moan,
Trying to drag the bugger back home.

Saw a drunk, thought he was dossin',
Lyin on a zebra crossin'
Drunk, he cried, 'Blast and dammer . . .
'Ow d'yer play this big pianner?'
Early one mornin' just at dawn,
Bloke doing press-ups on the lawn,
Drunk goin' home said, 'Ay 'up, son!
Don't you know the lass 'as gone!'

Is That the Moon?

Bright tempo

VERSES 1,2,3,4.

Late one night I was having some fun, Woke up in the morning

dressed as a nun! Oh Lord! I ain't gon-na drink,

Ain't gon-na drink no more Goin' through the park with a

pain in my head, Fighting the flowers for their beds.

Oh Lord! I ain't gonna drink, Ain't gonna drink no more - Oh me oh

CHORUS

my — I feel so high Is that the

moon — Or is it the sun up in the sky?

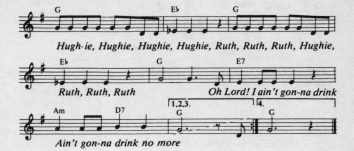

Hugh-ie, Hughie, Hughie, Hughie, Ruth, Ruth, Ruth, Hughie,

Ruth, Ruth, Ruth   Oh Lord! I ain't gon-na drink

Ain't gon-na drink no more

The Cock and the Ass

There was an old woman, a likely old lass,
Who took out her washing with a cart and an ass.
Every day her living to make,
This old woman her washing did take.

Chorus
To me fol de rol rol, fol de rol rol
Fol de rol, fol de rol, fol de rol day

There was also an old man whose knees they did knock,
Though a very old man, he'd a large Red Rhode Island cock.
One day this old woman she chanced to pass by,
His cock it jumped up and pecked out donkey's eye!
With me fol de rol rol, etc. . .

Oh the court chanced to meet the very next day,
So the woman she took him to court right away.
And the judge he sat there as stern as a rock,
And he said, 'Old lad, you'll pay dear for your cock.'
With me fol de rol rol, etc. . .

I'll fine you ten pounds, you nasty old man,
If you can't pay me now, you must pay when you can.
'Cos I think things have come to a very fine pass,
When you can't keep your cock from an old woman's ass,
With me fol de rol rol, etc. . .

The Cock and the Ass

Born Bad

Zeke McGinty was in trouble and he knew it. He looked at the ragged tyre on his bicycle and spat into the alkali dust. A lizard scuttled across the hot boulders into the shade. Zeke's eyes narrowed in his leathery tanned face as he looked over the butte towards the mesa. It was the first time he had been so far out into the Bad Lands; he'd been to the Not Very Good Lands and even passed through the Downright Rotten Lands but this was the first time he'd been out so far into the cruel burning canyons and gulches of the Black Hills. He was a good day's ride out from the ranch with no sandwiches or bus fare. No one would come looking for him for another day at least, maybe two hundred years and by that time he could be dead or very unhappy.

He took the saddle off his lamed bicycle and threw it on to the ground. The bicycle's front wheel spun list-lessly in the hot sun, casting spindly shadows on the baked earth. Zeke took out his .45 and cocked the trigger. He squinted down the sights at the little picture of Noddy on the bell.

'Goodbye, old friend,' he murmured, a lone tear streaking the dust on his tanned cheek. He squeezed the trigger. One spasmodic jerk of the brakes told him that his faithful steed had passed away.

As the day wore on, Zeke thought about the last few months. It had seemed like the beginning of a new life for him and Sarey Ann and little Clem. He had thrown up his job as an acupuncturist and part-time wall-of-death rider back East to hit the trail West with all the other hopefuls; some were running away from something, some were running towards something. Zeke was just running, curry had that effect on him. The trail was full of pioneers on their way to the virgin lands just opened up by the government after they'd bought them from the Indians for four tin-openers and a promise that their chief could have his picture on the front page of the *National Geographic Magazine*.

Zeke had staked his claim like everyone else and, at first, things had gone better than they could have hoped. The ranch-house roof had only blown off fourteen times and only eleven of their thirteen children had died of the fever or been carried off by bears while the bicycle ranch had risen in strength from thirty head to three thousand. The new railroad had opened up lines back East. It was a new country and people were clamouring for bicycles. It was all Zeke could do to breed them and break them in in time for sale. Things had looked real good for a while.

Then disaster had struck in the shape of the Kowalski sisters – a quartet of blowzy saloon bar dancers and delicatessen owners who wanted Zeke's land to build a matzoh ranch and a mazuzza factory. At first, they'd tried to use gentle persuasion, such as nibbling the lobes of his ears and rubbing their hands inside his shirt while showing him pictures of money, but he'd resisted them by wearing a Balaclava, and a roll-neck sweater and showing them pictures of the word 'No'.

Then the Kowalski sisters turned dirty. Zeke went out one morning to find that someone had lamed a couple of hundred of his bicycles and stolen the pumps off most of the others. Then a month later someone poisoned the drinking holes and the landscape was dotted with the bones and handlebars of his stock. Then, as a final stroke, someone had burned down the ranch and, as he was riding for help, his mount was lamed on some tin tacks and school compasses they'd laid on the track.

Zeke cursed his luck and spat on a lizard that was blinking at him in the dust. The lizard went and told a snake which came out and bit him. A ball of tumbleweed rolled towards him and broke both his legs. It wasn't Zeke's lucky day. Even the vultures were putting their bibs on and arguing about the seating plan.

As the sun rose higher above the arid lands the heat caused the air to shimmer and twitch until the landscape all about him looked like a nightmare land filled with phantoms and incredible grotesques. 'I didn't know you could get "Crossroads" out here,' thought Zeke.

So it was that at first Zeke had thought that the stranger riding towards him was another trick of the light. Out of the shimmering horizon he came, dressed all in white, with a black mask covering his eyes. He rode a snow-white bicycle while behind him on a palamino bicycle with Campagnolo gears and centrepull brakes, came a swarthy Plains Indian, riding bareback, with a squint. The last thing Zeke saw before he passed out was the stranger bending over him, smiling.

When he came to he was lying in a strange bed propped up on pillows. The stranger and the Indian were by the bedside. Zeke smiled weakly.

'You saved my life, stranger, I'm beholden to you.'

'Can you lend me five pounds?' asked the stranger.

'Sure,' whispered Zeke. 'How long have I been here?'

'Three weeks,' said the stranger. 'Say, you couldn't

make it ten pounds, could you?'

'Sure,' croaked Zeke, 'after all you saved my life, didn't you? But what about my ranch and my wife and children?'

'Ranch now matzoh factory and bagel-mine, already, my life keemo sabbi,' said the Indian, whose name was Tonto Finklestein. 'Wife now many moons' ride away, running magazine called *Dry Gulch Nudist Train-Spotter and Puzzlers News and Macrobiotic Bugle.*'

Zeke gulped back a sob.

'Can you make it fifty pounds by any chance?' asked the stranger, his face set in a compassionate leer.

'Take it all, my life is finished anyway,' groaned Zeke, throwing his wallet towards him.

'Ay up! Brass!!'* called the masked man, leaping on to his bicycle.

'Who was that masked man?' croaked Zeke, as they were lynching him next day for not being able to pay the hotel bill.

The minister looked up from his knitting and said softly, 'I don't rightly know but round these here parts they call him The Lone Sponger.'

*Not 'Hi-Ho Silver!' as is sometimes thought.

Born Bad

I was too poor to be born
So my momma had me knitted by the WVS,
And lookin' at me now, you know,
I think they was a ball of wool short, more or less!
Ma poppa was in prison
For printin' bits of paper with the Queen's head on;
And people said, 'Goddamn',
As ah smoked mah pot sat in mah pram, I wuz mah poppa's
    son.

I was so poor that mah dawg had no legs
And ah had to take him out when it wuz dark.
From the wrong side of the track
I'd carry him there and back,
Takin' him for a drag in the local park.

I stole the other babies' rattles,
Their dummies and their bottles and their chewin' bones.
Got hooked on teethin' jelly,
Got busted at the clinic when they found me stoned.
When I was five they made me go to school,
And all the other children there called me names
So I got some plaster of Paris
And put it in their milk and slowed down all their games.

Teacher told me I wuz no good
On the day I chopped the school down with my junior
    woodman's axe.
She didn't like me drinkin' ink
And gettin high on plasticine and melted crayon wax.
When I wuz seven I left home,
'Cos mah my girlfriend wuz in trouble and mah dog had bit the
    priest.
With mah guitar and mah bed-roll
Ah left Oldham bound for Nashville but mah mah had told the
    police.

So they dragged me off to prison
And left me here a-sittin' lookin at bars and locks;
And mah poor old doggie's dead
'Cos he ate a policeman's leg and choked on one of his socks.
And you know ah sit in here and wonder
How the Hell I came to get me in this mess,
An' I guess I got to blame it
On them goddam knittin' needles of the WVS.

Born Bad

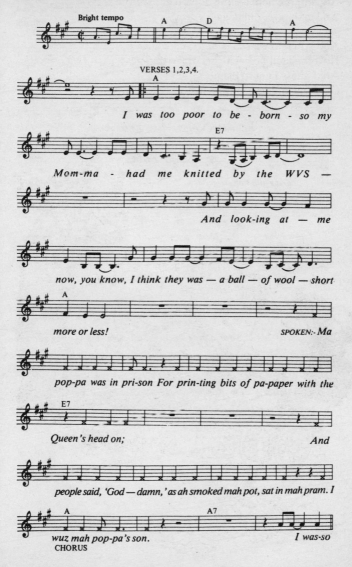

Bright tempo

A   D   A

VERSES 1,2,3,4.
A

I was too poor to be - born - so my

E7

Mom-ma - had me knitted by the WVS —

And look-ing at — me

now, you know, I think they was — a ball — of wool — short

A

more or less!   SPOKEN:- Ma

pop-pa was in pri-son For prin-ting bits of pa-paper with the

E7

Queen's head on;   And

people said, 'God — damn,' as ah smoked mah pot, sat in mah pram. I

A   A7

wuz mah pop-pa's son.   I was-so
CHORUS

poor that mah dog had no legs. And ah

had to take him out — when it — was dark.

From the wrong side of the track — I'd

car-ry him there and back, Tak-ing him for a

drag in the local park — I was born bad.

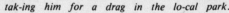

Tak-ing him for a drag in the lo-cal park — I was no good —

tak-ing him for a drag in the lo-cal park.

Away with Rum

We're coming, we're coming, our brave little band,
On the right side of Temperance we now take our stand!
We don't smoke tobacco because we do think
That the people who do so are likely to drink.

Chorus
Away, away with rum by gum!
With rum, by gum, with rum, by gum!
Away, away with rum, by gum,
That's the song of the Salvation Army.

We never have biscuits 'cos biscuits have yeast,
And too many bickies turns a man to a beast.
Can you imagine the utter disgrace
Of a man in the gutter with crumbs on his face?

We never have wine gums 'cos wine gums have port,
And too many wine gums make you do what you shouldn't
    ought.
Can you imagine confessing to dad,
'It was only them wine gums what made me go mad!'

We never use Brylcreem as that's got bay rum,
And too many rubbings can turn your head numb.
But here's a thought that will have you in fits –
Just imagine them millions of paralytic nits.

Now if you go hiking and get two sore feet,
Don't use surgical spirit though it cures 'em a treat,
'Cos it seeps through the pores by a process called osmosis,
And you end up by having ten drunk little toeses.

We never have crumpet 'cos crumpet's got grain,
And too many nibbles can drive you insane.
Can you imagine just sitting all night,
Nibbling a bit of crumpet until you get tight?

Away with Rum

CHORUS

A - way, a - way with rum, by gum! With rum, by gum, with rum, by gum! A - way, a - way, with rum, by gum, That's the song of the Sal-va-tion Ar - my.

Opt. vamp - under chat

Opt. repeat of vamp

Chat ad lib

We

VERSES

ne-ver have bis-cuits, 'cause bis-cuits have yeast, And too ma-ny bic-kies turns a man to a beast. Can you i-ma-gine the ut-ter dis-grace Of a man ly-ing in the gut-ter with crumbs on his face? — A tight A

To Coda

D.S. al Coda

For repeat

Last time

CODA

song of the Sal-va-tion Ar — my.

Fine

The Man Who Bangs the Button

The mechanistic view of life proposed by behaviourists like B. F. Skinner asserts that we are all merely sets of conditioned reflexes with no free will. As he sees it, everything that happens to us from the cradle to the grave conditions us so that there is no possibility of us reacting to any event in any way other than that ordained by our conditioning. The arrival of saints, criminals, idiots, politicians, wars and other man-made disasters on the face of the Earth could all be forecast given that all the known facts could be assembled and fed into the computer.

There was a bloke like Skinner in Blackpool once, called Sigismund Makepiece Boil. He had a factory that made Blackpool Rock – rock in every shape, colour and size. Rock shaped like babies' dummies, bottles of Blue Bass, ladies' breasts, dentists' fingers; rock in every hue of the spectrum and several that hadn't even been thought of yet. But his speciality, his *pièce de resistance,* his brainchild, was rock with A PRESENT FROM BLACKPOOL written all the way through it.

The man who put the letters in the sticks of Blackpool Rock was Ezekial Phlegm, the natural son of a Puerto Rican elastic-band designer and a Barnsley spare-part surgeon. The spare-part surgeon from Barnsley had the rare distinction of being the only man who had stood on one hand before Queen Victoria while juggling a dozen live hedgehogs with his bare feet and shouting the *Song of Solomon* up his trouser leg, a feat that earned him twelve guineas, the royal patronage and a severe hernia.

Ezekial Phlegm was married to his work – Ethel Hiswork – a large woman of Romany extraction (she blackmailed gypsies). Ethel supplemented the family income by dressing up in feathers, tying a rope round her waist and arranging for the Corporation to drag her along the Mersey tunnel as a pull-through.

Ezekial loved his job, working late into the night in his house behind the freak show with the man-eating budgie and the octopus girl in her four pairs of fish-net tights. There, all alone, his bony fingers weaved the intricate letters in and out of the miles of sticky toffee. The only cloud on his horizon was Sigismund Boil. He was so tight, his purse screamed when he opened it and he still had shares in the South Sea Bubble.

One day Sigismund Boil swept into the toffee factory, his face as dark as the inside of a cow's bum, and just as attractive.

'Now then, tha knows trouble at t'mill. Where there's brass, there's muck! Eee! Sithee! By 'eck! I want twenty more per miles per rock per week and you'll do it for half per brass in more per muck . . . so think on!'

So saying, he threw a bag of manure on the floor and walked out across the ceiling. He was a fly old devil!

Ezekial settled down to his work with a sigh, writing A PRESENT FROM BLACKPOOL in 170 miles of rock with an extremely long pen. He had the look on his face of a man resigned to his fate which was a good job because nobody else wanted it.

Next pay day at exactly the same time, like some bad fairy godfather, Sigismund Boil reappeared, muttering loudly, 'Where there's brass, there's muck . . . there's the muck . . . see if you can find the brass in it.' He threw another bag of manure on the floor, shouting, 'And think on. I want another per two thousand miles per rock per week and for one quarter per money!!' So saying, he stormed out, taking the window with him, leaving the room in darkness.

'You're a hard master, Mr Boil,' murmured Ezekial, as he turned his head back towards the rock-lettering bench.

Hardly had he said this than the door opened and Sigismund Boil reappeared, carrying a whip which he used to threaten the toffee-maker with.

'Hands up, Phlegm! I heard that . . . a hard master eh! Well, be careful, Phlegm – this whip is loaded and I'm a violent man. I'll show you how hard I can be . . . I want per ten thousand miles per rock by Friday . . . or I shall go round to your house and break up all your toys!!'

The poor toffee-maker threw himself on the floor wringing his hands, but nobody answered because they were all out. He pleaded but it was no use. Sigismund Boil, apprentice pantomime villain, stormed out taking the door with him. There was no escape.

Night and day, day and night, the poor rock-maker worked, his fingernails ragged and torn, his breath coming quick then slow, then quick-quick then slow. . . . Cribbens! his lungs were doing the quickstep on their own! As he dotted the last 'i' in Blackpool* his frail heart gave way, and there in the little hut behind the freak show, Ezekial Phlegm died of death and Come Dancing of the lungs.

The next morning found Sigismund Boil a sadder and

* People have pointed out that there is no 'i' in Blackpool but there must be because you can't dot 'o's.

a wiser man. Sadder not at the fate of Ezekial Phlegm but at the sight of ten thousand miles of Blackpool Rock with, along its entire length in a practised hand, the immortal legend, SIGISMUND BOIL IS A BAG OF SHIT!

Inside all of us somewhere there is a little of the revolutionary, the anarchist, a little Ezekial Phlegm, even perhaps inside all of us** a little Ned Ludd.

** especially Mrs Ludd.

The Man Who Bangs the Button

Every morning at seven o'clock,
Mr Dailygrind walks round the block
To go and bang the button that makes all the
    wheels go round.
With the prospect of a gold wrist watch,
For twenty-five years he's turned the block
To go and bang the button that makes all the
    wheels go round.
Day after day his life slips away,
As he fills his dreams with impossible schemes,
Minding the machine
That makes the plastic submarines
That you find in your cornflakes every day.

Lives with his mother in Paradise Flats,
With a budgie called Peter and a marmalade cat.
The man who bangs the button that makes all the wheels go
    round.
Forty years old and never been kissed,
Doesn't drink, doesn't smoke, doesn't know what he's missed.
Just bangs the button that makes all the wheels go round.
His mother and he sit watchin' TV,
As he sees the world pass
Through the rented glass,
Mr Average man
Fits in with the plan,
Guaranteed not to make waves.

But romance came to Dailygrind,
As he sat there watching the flickering dials,
Banging the button that makes all the wheels go round,
In the unlikely shape of Ermentrude Green
Who wheeled the tea urn from the works canteen
To the man who bangs the button that makes all the wheels go
    round.
She gave him a smile and completely beguiled him,
This unwise virgin
What needed no urgin'.
She gave him a look
Across a cracked cup,
She was an oasis in an otherwise sexual desert.

He passed her a note in his empty mug
Saying, 'My heart for you burns with love,
I'll bang your button and make all your wheels go round,
I'll wait for you at the factory gates,
Please, my tea lady, don't be late.
I'll bang your button and make all your wheels go round.'
So their love bloomed

Through May and June;
They were happy and smiled
Through the whole of July.
He sat at his machine
Making plastic submarines,
And mucky thoughts ran through his mind.

Till one day, as he waited for tea,
She passed him a note where plain to see
Was, 'Dear man who bangs the button that makes all the
    wheels go round,
I know this may sound very hard,
But it's the boss now that clocks me card,
Not the man who bangs the button that makes all the wheels go
    round.'
He stared at the page, his mind in a rage,
His jealousy churned,
And his nerve-ends burned.
And there and then,
This most average of men
Grabbed a spanner and moved to the machine.

Smash, bang, wallop, the cogwheels flew,
As Dailygrind the spanner threw,
Jammed all the buttons that make all the wheels go round,
And faster and faster went the old machines
Spewing out millions of plastic submarines.
He'd buggered up the button that makes all the wheels go
    round,
And off he ran like a newborn man,
Did a bunk,
Got glorious drunk,
Packed his bags,
Left Paradise Flats,
And told them all to go and kiss his bum.

And they couldn't stop those old machines,
They went on pumpin' out submarines,
As the lights all flickered and the wheels went whizzing round,
They filled the works from the roof to the floor
And went on pumpin' out the door,
Jammed all the streets and stopped all the traffic in town.
And miles away
In a field of hay,
Old Dailygrind,
Smashed out of his mind,
In the evening sunshine
With a bottle of wine,
He lay smiling at the birds and the trees.

The Man Who Bangs the Button

schemes,

Mind-ing the mach-ine That makes the

plastic sub-mar-ines _That you_ _find in your cornflakes ev-'ry_

[1,2,3,4,5,6. **Bright tempo** | 7.

INSTR.

_d a y ._

Bloomin' Grownups

They tell you not to play out late,
To be in bed by half-past eight,
Then they crawl home when daylight breaks,
Eyes like cuts in a pig's bum.

They make you eat up all your greens,
Cabbages and sprouts and runner beans,
But things that they don't like they leave,
They say it gives 'em the trotters.

They tell you everything you want's too dear,
And that you'll 'ave to wait another year,
Then they spend a fortune on fags and beer
And blame the Common Market.

We get a thump if me and our kid fight
And get sent to bed while it's still daylight,
But when they row they're at it all flippin' night,
Keepin' half the street up.

I got a crack off me dad for bein' rude (I said 'willy')
But if a bird's on the telly in the nude
To the TV screen his eyes are glued.
He says it's culture
(But culture doesn't make you dribble).

They throw your sweets and chocolates away,
It's bad for your health, that's what they say,
Then they smoke forty Park Drive a day,
Coughin' bits of lung up.

They tell you you should always tell the truth,
And if you tell a lie they hit the roof.
Then they try and pretend they like me Aunty Ruth
And slag her when her back's turned.

They tell you you should always be well dressed
And be smart and clean and do your best,
Then me dad lies on the sofa in his braces and his vest,
Snorin' with his teeth out.
(Looks like a frog's bum.)

I just can't wait to be grown up,
They do what they like and never own up,
They bend all the rules, they've got it all sewn up,
Worse than the bloomin' Mafia.

Bloomin' Grownups

VERSES 1,2,3

They tell you not to play out late, to

be in bed by half past eight. Then they crawl home when daylight

breaks; eyes like cuts in a pig's bum. They

make you eat up all your greens, Cab-bages, sprouts and run-ner

beans, But things that they don't like they

leave.
CHORUS 1,2,3
They say it gives 'em the trot-ters. They

tell you every-thing you want's too dear, And

that you'll have to wait another year. Then they spend a for-tune on

fags and beer, And blame the Com-mon Mar-ket.

I think they're bloomin' bar-my.

The Ballad of Arnold Moon

Farting has not always been one of those physical activities that 'polite people' neither owned up to nor mentioned. Chaucer used to revel in it, making his characters let fly at every possible opportunity, while the diarists of the eighteenth and nineteenth centuries who staggered from one colossal feast to another must have been walking cannonades. Below are some excerpts from *The Diary of Samuel Poops,* an eighteenth-century diarist and a great lecher, trencherman and wine-bibber.

Nov. 12th

Up betimes with a head like a Papist's dog caused by too much of Mr Steven's port. Did let rip 7vral tymes at ye breakfast table – one so bad ye dog slunke out of ye room, frothinge and whinninge. To Lord Scrotum's* this noon where we dined for 7vral hours on a roast goose, a hog, 7vral capons cold, a large cheese, some boiled mutton spiced with cloves, boiled sprouts, leeks and peas and a side of venison. Did washe it down with 7vral bottles of good sack and a few of port. Some of ye ruder fellows 'gan to let off and did light them with

---

* Lord Scrotum – a wrinkled retainer.

tapers causing much hallooing and whooping. One of ye maids did come in to see what was ye merriment and did fall down in a faint to see ye flames leaping from Lord Scrotum's pantaloons, so I did ravish her. Squire Jameson did suffer a blow back of ye flames and did almost cook his trypes. A surgeon had to be sent for who pronounced them singed but serviceable. Did fart all ye way home in ye coach until ye coachman put me out by ye Fleet saying I did frighten his horse. Walked home hitting beggars on ye way. And so to bed.

Dec. 13th

Awake all night with ye blue squitters and ye groaning trotters, caused by a peppery eel pie I consumed for supper. I physiked myself with raw eggs and rum mixed with sour cream, pickled onions and some lemon. Breakfasted on half a lamb cold, and a gallon of Rhenish wine, mulled, some cold leeks stewed, and a pease pudding. Ravished ye maid.

To see ye play, *Volpone,* this aft. Farted all ye way through Act 2 and did cause much merriment. Ye man Jonson is a fule and writes like a tailor. Saw him after at Lord Snatcher's and told him so.

'Sir,' I said, 'you write like a tailor!'

'And you, sir, fart like a Papist,' he returned, which I thought very saucy. Did ravish Lord Snatcher's maid on the stairs for she has breasts like ripe Stiltons.

This evening dined at my house with ye Lord Privy Seal, ye Lord High Admiral and General Foxe on a side of venison, a jugged hare, some cold beef, some pressed mutton, an ox's sweetbreads, 7vral dishes of leeks and onions, two large Stiltons and 7vral bottles of madeira. General Foxe did gette so merrie he did piddle on ye fire and fall down. Ye Lord High Admiral so full of drink that he talked to ye curtains for a good half hour believing them to be me. I ravished ye maid again while ye Lord Privy Seal drank from his boot. General Foxe did try to fart in tune in ye manner of ye Spaniards but only succeeded in giving himself a squint and bursting a blood vessel on his nose. Ye Lord High Admiral very drunk did fall with his head in ye cheese and did think we had put the candles out.

My Lords and I laughed at ye story of Lady M. who did let off a ripper before ye king and did seek to hide it by saying it was a cough.

'A cough, madam!' he did say. 'Then pray loosen your undergarments for methinks they are too tight about your throat.'

General Foxe laughed very hearty at ye jeste and vowed that he liked it so much he would get up and piddle on ye fire again, which he did, putting it out. And so to bed.

The Ballad of Arnold Moon

There once was a man called Arnold Moon,
Found that he could fart in tune.
People came from miles around
Just to hear old Arnold play
Rock and roll and razzamatazz,
Old time classical, even jazz.
Never knew he was sittin' on a gold-mine;
Just did it for the pleasure it gave.

But his ill wind it blew no good,
And a bloke turned up at Arnold's pub,
Said he was a talent scout
Come to hear old Arnold play.
So he did some bluegrass, 'Blowin' in the Wind',
A fugue by Bach and 'My Ding-a-Ling',
Finished off with 'Stormy Weather',
And they all stood for The Queen.

Well, the talent scout he was knocked out:
'If people can stand the smell,' he shouts,
'I'll make you a star, there is no doubt!
Just sign on this dotted line.'
So the scout he took him a piece of Moon,
Got him an agent, and very soon
He'd got him a manager and a roadie too
To carry the tins of beans!

He showed his face in all the places,
Showed his place to all the faces,
Got him a big recording deal;
And a man from Milan who taught him scales
Made him practise all the day,
Fed him mushy peas and wet hay.
You could hear him miles away
When he played the 1812!

There was money for the gear, money for the van,
And pretty soon that poor old man
Had him seventeen bodyguards
And a doctor in case he got a sore throat!
There was so many in for their per cent
He never knew where the money all went,
But he kept half London in food and rent
Just by fartin' in tune.

All his records got to the top,
He did Wagner's *Ring* on 'Top of the Pops',
Nobody thought that the money would stop
Rolling, rolling, rolling in.
Then word it spread throughout the land
They'd booked Arnold Moon for a Royal Command
The press it really went to town
Front-page in all the news!
(Spoken) Ace to trump before Queen
Will there be a Royal Flush.

The TV and the radio
They were there for the Royal Show;
All the lights began to glow
As Arnold Moon he took the stage.
Then all his nightmares they came true
When he got a follow-through
In the middle of the 'Flight of the Bumble Bee'
And filled the stage with cccccccccc. . . .

The Ballad of Arnold Moon

A Sailor Courted a Farmer's Daughter

'Hope beats eternal in the human trousers' – *Casanova*

'Love makes the world go round' according to ninety per cent of modern songs and 'All the world loves a lover' (except the men who have to come and unblock the drains). If Love is so loved then nothing is more guaranteed to tug at the heart-strings of the world than a love-song.

This love-song was written by Dr Elphinstone J. Drinkpootle in 1726. Drinkpootle was a quack, mendicant friar and mountebank who became prime minister of England for two hours in 1723 due to a total misunderstanding when he went into the House of Commons out of the rain. Drinkpootle was a little under average height, standing only four feet two inches in his bare feet, a fact that caused him great embarrassment and which he tried to remedy by filling his boots with manure and sleeping on a rack. When this didn't work he had scaffolding made for his legs and constructed a special pair of steam dancing feet which exploded one evening in the Pump Room at Bath causing the death of seventeen people. Drinkpootle only escaped the lynch-mob that formed after the disaster by disguising himself as an

127

organ-grinder's monkey and posting himself to Lincoln-shire, where he spent the rest of his days running a coaching house called the Frog and Toothpuller.

This inn became a famous haunt of thieves, highway-men, brigands, cutpurses, pirates and insurance men, and Drinkpootle became well known as one of the most famous innkeepers of all time. He was a man of prodigious strength and is reputed to have had navel muscles so strong that he could crack Brazil nuts and open bottles of small beer with his belly-button. For a wager once he opened a hundred and seventeen oysters with his navel and for an encore peeled an orange with his hands behind his back.

Drinkpootle also perfected the old North Country traditional sport of ear wrestling, where two strong men, locked together right ear to right ear, would each attempt to push the other's nose into a bowl of live crabs, lighted candles and tin tacks. His nose bore the scars of many a duel and 'as lumpy as Drinkpootle's nose' was a phrase used to describe porridge, fog and serving wenches' thighs in the inns of the Great North Road.

'A Sailor Courted a Farmer's Daughter' comes from a novel written by Elphinstone J. Drinkpootle – *The Curse of Black Eric and his dog Reg* – a pirate story set in the Caribbean and Barnsley. Black Eric is a fierce pirate with a patch over his ear and a wooden nose, who ends his horrific career at Tyburn on a charge of piracy, murder and failing to return his library books.

Here is an excerpt from *The Curse of Black Eric and his dog Reg:*

Black Eric lowered his spyglass and spat a thin yellow stream of tobacco juice through the gap between his gums.

'Blast and belay and look limber, ye crew of yellow maggots!' he growled, 'tis a cargo ship, the *Limping*

128

Vicar, outward bound from Kingston. All hands on deck and them with no hands throw yer stumps!!!' Black Eric spat another stream of tobacco juice and called, 'Get ready to board her, Mr Mate!'

'Aye aye, Cap'n, called the mate, walking over the ship's rail into the sea, his eyes full of tobacco juice.

'Jenkins, you're the mate now,' snarled Black Eric, pointing at a one-eyed pirate with no teeth, no hair, no ears or nose and a face so covered in cutlass scars that when he closed his eyes he looked like a steam pudding in a string bag.

Jenkins farted loudly.

'I told ye to do that on the poop deck,' growled Black Eric, spitting out another stream of tobacco juice.

'Aye aye, Cap'n,' answered Jenkins, walking over the ship's rail into the sea, his eyes full of tobacco juice.

Three mates later the ships crunched together, as Black Eric gave the command to board her and the cabin boy ran a teatowel and a pair of braces to the top of the mast.

'Yer supposed to run up the skull and crossbones, ye little ship's biscuit,' snarled Black Eric, cracking his skull with a belaying pin.

'I can't see it, Cap'n, my eyes are full of tobacco juice,' said the cabin boy walking off the deck into the sea.

There was a cry of despair from the *Limping Vicar* as the dreaded skull and crossbones fluttered in the breeze and the sky grew dark with flying grappling irons and love notes from the homosexuals hoping for a bit of a change. In minutes the battle was over and with the decks awash with blood, TCP and Elastoplast, the two captains exchanged names and addresses and insurance particulars, as the cooks of both ships went down below to show each other the Golden Rivet.

'I thought you said Golden Privet!' said one galley boy, but it was too late.

A Sailor Courted a Farmer's Daughter

A sailor courted a farmer's daughter (Nyaaaar)
That lived contagious unto the town of Straban,
With melody and woe he did besought her
That she'd marry himself before any other type, kind, species
   or classification of a man.

Now this farmer's daughter she had fine possess-i-ons,
A silver teapot and three pounds fifteen and sixpence all in
    gold. (Nyaaaar)
Oh, marry me quick, me salt seawater sailor!
Before I make a big big bundleen of my fine possess-i-ons,
And throw them all deep down into the waters stinking and
    cold and full of dead dogs and old prams and frogspawn
    down below.

Oh, I'd marry you, me heartless conchantlement,
If ye'd nothin' at all at all to keep the ould hens of
 Knockmachree from tearing down the house about your ears
 but your old wan's curse. (Nyaaaar)
So she made a big bundle of her fine possess-i-ons
And threw them deep down into the bottom of the ocean cold
 and stinking and full of the dead dogs and frog spawn that
 was in it . . . (that ends that verse)

Now the sailor he could swim like a duckeen,
And diving down into the bottom of the ocean full of dead dogs
 and ould bedspreads and prams and mangles down below,
 (Nyaaaar)
Didn't he? wasn't he after? He did and he was – comin' up with
 the bundle all smiling and a chucklin',
Thinkin' of the great times he'd have when he got back home to
 his Uncle Eric and cousin Maureen and Spot the dog away
 back in Ballinasloe.

Now the farmer's daughter near widdled herself laughin',
For there was nothing in the bundle at all but an ould
 putcheenian of a stone!
A sailor courted a farmer's daughter
And now he wished he'd left the dirty ould bitch alone.

A Sailor Courted a Farmer's Daughter

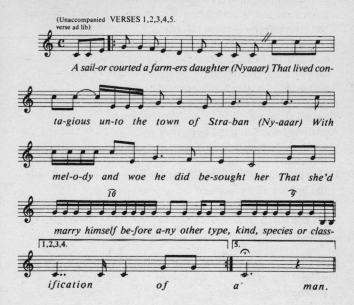

(Unaccompanied VERSES 1,2,3,4,5.
verse ad lib)

A sail-or courted a farm-ers daughter (Nyaaar) That lived con-ta-gious un-to the town of Stra-ban (Ny-aaar) With mel-o-dy and woe he did be-sought her That she'd marry himself be-fore a-ny other type, kind, species or class-ification of a man.

Acknowledgements

Most of the songs in this collection are my own words and music. The others I learnt from various people when I was tearing up and down the country doing the round of the folk clubs and festivals of this fair land, and I'd like to thank: Paul Graney, folk-song collector and freedom fighter in Spain and elsewhere, for 'The German Clockwinder' and 'The Keyhole in the Door'; Mick Heywood of Batley for 'The Cock and the Ass', learnt from him over many a pint in the Star and Elsinore, Whitby; Tony Downes for 'A Sailor Courted a Farmer's Daughter', and Frank Duffy for 'Away With Rum'.

Discography

Over the years I have committed several of my mean-derings on to wax and some of them are still available for those stout of heart. Don't play them while the vicar's there!

A Lancashire Lad
(Transatlantic Records LER 2039) includes:
'The German Clockwinder'
'The Keyhole in the Door'
'The Hattersley Lament'
'The Cock and the Ass'

Mrs 'Ardin's Kid
(Rubber Records RUB 011) includes:
'Away with Rum'
'A Sailor Courted a Farmer's Daughter'
'The Drunken Tackler'

Old Four Eyes is Back
(Philips 6308 290) includes:
'Born Bad'

On The Touchline
(Philips 9109 230) includes:
'The Man Who Bangs the Button'
'St George Doesn't Live Here Anymore'

Postscript

I was just an ordinary child, living out a simple life in the sleepy backwaters of Manchester. The world seemed to drift by tirelessly like a meandering river while we on its banks watched, simple and contented. Then one day the circus came to town with its tumbling clowns and spangled ladies, its strong men and ferocious leopards. In the winking of an eye, the great marquee went up and in the gloom of that November night we threaded our way across the crofts following the bright, coloured lights, the throbbing of the generators and the heady smell of the greasepaint and sawdust. That night my life was transformed utterly . . . from then on I knew what I wanted to be . . . a sea lion.

MIKE HARDING
Madame Olroyd's Home for The Incurably Optimistic, Barnsley

THE UNLUCKIEST MAN IN THE WORLD
and similar disasters

Mike Harding

Born in the picturesque spa of Lower Crumpsall, he spent his early years in the brooding shadow of a cream cracker factory. At the age of seventeen he bought a set of Mongolian bagpipes and joined a rock and roll band. Much of his manhood has been spent waiting for a girl wearing red feathers and a hulu skirt to come into his life. He is the incorrigible, irrepressible and slightly mad Mike Harding.

The Unluckiest Man in the World takes us into the world of Mike Harding with an inimitable collection of happy, sad, ridiculous, profound and simply hilarious songs, poems and stories.

A LITTLE ZIT ON THE SIDE

Jasper Carrott

He's been a delivery boy (the terror of Solihull), a toothpaste salesman (for four hours), a folkie (repertoire – two songs) – and the most unlikely and original comic superstar for years.

Now Jasper Carrott reveals more of the outrageous talent that has taken him from the Boggery to a series of one-man shows that won him ITV's Personality of the Year Award.

Discover the do-it-yourself man, how to become star of Top of the Pops and the Carrott guide to dog-training. Relive the simple pleasures of The Magic Roundabout, Funky Moped and the Mole.

TALES FROM A LONG ROOM

Peter Tinniswood

Those were the golden days: WG and Spofforth were locked in mortal combat at Lord's; MCC rule held sway throughout the Empire; and the world had not yet been darkened by the spectre of aluminium bats, Geoffrey Boycott and underarm bowling.

The brigadier remembers it all. By the flickering firelight of a long room, he takes us back to some surprisingly little-known incidents and characters from cricket's heyday. It's all here – the MCC's ill-fated Test against a Pygmy XI, Scott and Amundsen's historic match at the South Pole, the inspiring story of Mendip-Hughes, Somerset's most distinguished one-legged off-spinner, and, of course, the promising but tragically short career in first-class cricket of the late Queen Victoria.

Tales from a Long Room is the tallest, most hilarious collection of stories in the history of the 'summer game'.

GULLIBLE'S TRAVELS

Billy Connolly

He has travelled from the majestic deserts of Doha (twin town of Drumchapel in Scotland) and the teeming markets of Bletchley to the splendour of the Sydney surf and the exotic decadence of the Crawley Leisure Centre.

And here it is — a unique guide to the world, travel, life, death and camel-smells, as seen through the eyes of

'the gangling Glaswegian doyen of bad taste' *Daily Telegraph*

'the man who makes Bette Midler look like Jess Conrad' *The Stage*

'one of the most outrageous Scotsmen ever to have vaulted Hadrian's Wall' *Daily Express*

'the laughing laureate of the loo' *The Times*

the inimitable (thank God) BILLY CONNOLLY

Compiled by Duncan Campbell

Illustrated by Steve Bell

THE DIETER'S GUIDE TO WEIGHT LOSS DURING SEX

Richard Smith

Tired? Listless? Overweight? Open this book at any page and discover everything you wanted to know about sex, food and dieting but never dreamt of asking.

Activity	Calories burned
REMOVING CLOTHES	
With partner's consent	12
Without partner's consent	187
Unhooking bra	
Using two calm hands	7
Using one trembling hand	96
EMBARRASSMENT	
Large juice stain on shorts	10
ORGASM	
Real	27
Faked	160

(Continued on page 81)

BESTSELLING HUMOUR BOOKS
FROM ARROW

All these books are available from your bookshop or news-
agent or you can order them direct. Just tick the titles you
require and complete the form below.

☐	THE ASCENT OF RUM DOODLE	W. E. Bowman	£1.75
☐	THE COMPLETE NAFF GUIDE	Bryson, Fitzherbert and Legris	£2.50
☐	SWEET AND SOUR LABRADOR	Jasper Carrott	£1.75
☐	GULLIBLE'S TRAVELS	Billy Connolly	£1.95
☐	THE MALADY LINGERS ON	Les Dawson	£1.25
☐	A. J. WENTWORTH	H. F. Ellis	£1.60
☐	THE CUSTARD STOPS AT HATFIELD	Kenny Everett	£1.75
☐	BUREAUCRATS — HOW TO ANNOY THEM	R. T. Fishall	£1.50
☐	THE ART OF COARSE RUGBY	Michael Green	£1.95
☐	THE ARMCHAIR ANARCHIST'S ALMANAC	Mike Harding	£1.95
☐	CHRISTMAS ALREADY?	Gray Jolliffe	£1.25
☐	THE JUNKET MAN	Christopher Matthew	£1.75
☐	FILSTRUP FLASHES AGAIN	Peter Plant	£1.25
☐	A LEG IN THE WIND	Ralph Steadman	£1.75
☐	TALES FROM A LONG ROOM	Peter Tinniswood	£1.75

Postage ———

Total ———

ARROW BOOKS, BOOKSERVICE BY POST, PO BOX 29,
DOUGLAS, ISLE OF MAN, BRITISH ISLES

Please enclose a cheque or postal order made out to Arrow Books Ltd
for the amount due including 15p per book for postage and packing
both for orders within the UK and for overseas orders.

Please print clearly

NAME ....

ADDRESS ....

....

Whilst every effort is made to keep prices down and to keep popular
books in print, Arrow Books cannot guarantee that prices will be the
same as those advertised here or that the books will be available.